203

TRAVEL CHALLENGES

203 TRAVEL CHALLENGES
TRAVEL THE WORLD. EXPLORE YOUR INNER SELF.

ISBN: 978-619-7198-99-7

Delivering professional book publishing and distribution services BGKniga Plc. is not interfering in authors' creative processes and does not bear responsibility for the content of the book published under the Fabrika za knigi imprint.

© Maria Angelova, author
© Ivalina Nenova, author
© Irina Peneva, illustrations
© Nikolina Ruskova, translation
© James Crouchman, editor
© Lucy Mallows, editor
© A+A /Alexandra Dimitrova, Asen Nenov/, graphic design

Contents

In today's world, we read more and more but actually learn less and less. We travel more but change less. We watch more but play a smaller part in our own lives. We've seen infinite tourist destinations a thousand times on the Internet and no longer are easily amazed, even when we actually visit the place. So why do we bother to travel at all?

The book you're holding is different to any travel book you've read until now. It's not for reading, it's for taking action. It will give you ideas for destinations and new experiences but, above all, it will challenge you to do, see, hear and try things you've never thought of doing while traveling. It will force you to open your mind to all the exciting opportunities you have and rarely use. It will inspire you to transform every trip into your very own personal adventure.

Who is this book for?

For anyone who thinks they have tried everything (most challenges appear in several variants with different levels of difficulty, intended for different types of travelers). For anyone who feels afraid of trying out new things (because there is a section called "How to do it" with instructions and specific ideas). For anyone who thinks they just can't (because there is a section called "Gain inspiration from..." filled with true stories of ordinary people, who will show you that you can actually do anything!). For any ordinary person who loves traveling, the new things in life as well as life itself. For any tired, busy, serious, conservative, disappointed or sad person - you are the one who needs a little change of scenery the most!

How to use this book?

Open it at a random page or choose among the sections in the book regarding topics. Read the challenge. Complete the challenge. Challenge a friend to fulfill the same task or open at a random page for a new idea.

We have left blank spaces in some parts of the book, where you can pose a personal challenge to yourself. Writing it down is important because it reminds you of your dreams and, little by little, transforms them into goals, only to become a reality. If we have forgotten something - write it in the margins, between the lines, across the illustrations - this book has been created for plans and ideas!
Do at least one thing you have never done before in your life - and you won't be able to stop. Take the ingredients of the challenges, stir them, move them and change them to create your own challenges.

Share your challenge, challenge somebody else

Share one of the challenges you've completed and become an inspiration to others. Send a story and a couple of photos to the dedicated website www.203challenges.com

or find more travel stories, inspired by the book. Share photos, thoughts, videos and texts on social networks. Sharing adventures is like a night around the campfire - it brings people closer in no time and creates a community of courageous, positive people, open to the world. You are one of those people.

Why exactly 203 challenges?

This is not another „101-beautiful-places-to-visit-in-your-life book". It's not about the number, it's not about the places, it's all about you. So we poured all of our souls, experience and inspiration into this guidebook. When we were done, the challenges turned out to be 203. The number was odd and somewhat arbitrary-looking but it turned out to be lucky (we consulted a Buddhist monk about it!).

We know you won't complete all challenges, and we know you will think of your own, and as this is meant to be a personal book, the final number actually depends on you.

TEST
What kind of traveler are you?

This test will give you useful, funny and interesting ideas on how to make your travels more enjoyable, according to your own personal interests.

There are no right or wrong answers. Just tick the

statement which most accurately describes your preferences. (At least at this stage of your life... with time these may change[1]). The test has been specifically designed for this book by the psychologist Ilina Nacheva. Be honest!

1. You often write down:
☼ ideas and thoughts that come to you out of the blue;
🍃 future tasks or information you will need later.

2. When communicating at work:
☀ you prefer to speak in person;
◊ you prefer emails - short and to the point.

3. You go out for dinner. You prefer:
🍃 to have an idea where you are going and with whom;
☼ to go out and decide as you go.

4. It's your birthday and you are holding a wrapped present. You feel most happy when:
🍃 you know it's something you chose;
☼ you have no idea what's inside, you simply enjoy the excitement of the surprise.

5. When you get together with friends:
◊ you usually just listen to group discussions and prefer to speak to people individually;
☀ you often end up as the center of everyone's attention.

---

1 Having mentioned that, here's challenge #204: do the same test in two years' time and compare the results. What is new about you and your life? How many trips did you experience and what were they like?

6. A personal or family holiday is coming soon. You prefer:

☼ to improvise - you know you will manage even in unexpected situations;

🍃 to plan ahead in order to organize the perfect event.

7. What makes you feel tense:

🍃 constant changes;

☼ monotony and routine.

8. People around you would most likely describe you as:

◌ a calm, quiet and reserved person;

☀ an active person, the life and soul of the party.

9. For you creating new contacts:

☀ happens often, it's easy and quick;

◌ takes some time and happens only when you need to.

10. Is it true that you need only four to five close friends?

◌ I would say it's true;

☀ I already have many close friends in my life. And I need all of them.

Results	🍃 . . . . . .
Next to each of the symbols mark the number of corresponding answers. **The two most frequent symbols will tell you what kind of traveler you are.**	☀ . . . . . .
	◌ . . . . . .
	☼ . . . . . .

The Organized Traveler

Researching your travels in advance is part of the adventure for you. Because you're good at organizing stuff, people often rely on you to choose the place for a holiday or a trip. They turn to you for advice and are happy to listen to your many travel stories.

You possess the unique ability to feel positive only at the thought of an upcoming journey, as long as you have formed your ideas and expectations.

It is important for you to be well aware in advance of things like environment, prices, location. When you arrive in a town you haven't been to before, you usually know exactly what you want to see... Right?

Recipe: Your perfect trip

Take people you like (the more the merrier).

Talk to other travelers in advance, collect recommendations for nice places and events - this way you will be sure you've seen everything worth seeing.

You will probably find it useful to make a list of your baggage items (so that you don't miss anything important).

Think about the things that will be useful in unexpected situations: road maps, travel insurance, phrase books of the local language, etc. Many people omit these details but it's always good to consider them for your own peace of mind!

Use your strengths while traveling: You are able to plan and organize the trip for the whole group - you have what it takes. Your natural talents step in when it's necessary to make lists of things to buy, to coordinate people and tasks before setting off. The role of a leader or a tour guide also suits you as seeking out information comes so effortlessly to you. When you need to negotiate at the hotel or socialize with the locals - again you are the right person because you are great at communicating. Last but not least, your ability to think ahead will come in very handy when packing bags and equipment.
Travel with friends, no matter where to!

What is the best way to approach this book?
Start from the very beginning - with the introduction and the "Who is this book for" section. Go through the contents and choose the chapter which seems most appealing to you and your travel companions (we don't know why but we have the feeling that you often travel in a group with other people).

When you find a challenge you like, spare some time for additional research. Probably the information about places and activities in this book will spark your curiosity for more details.
Mark the triumphant moment of completing the challenge

in a way you find best - film it, photograph it, write a travel story, post an article in a blog or simply post something short - this way you can share the experience with friends and close ones!

You can also get a copy of the book for your family/friends - this way you will read it together and exchange opinions and experience.

The Zen Traveler

To a large extent, traveling for you is an inner experience. The noise, the crowds and the small talk with strangers are all things you don't need to have a good time. On the contrary, you appreciate the charm of tucked-away villages and small towns. You tend to drift away with your thoughts and you often feel best in tranquil settings. You are not a fan of unforeseen surprises, you are more into experiences which are conveniently organized and prefer to stick to your own plan.

Also, we see you close to nature, indulging in the sound of your favorite music, book, sport, hobby or... simply oriented towards your inner self.

Recipe: Your perfect trip

Make enough time for preparation - no unnecessary last-minute tension.

If possible, choose an activity and destination which allow for personal space.

Do research in advance so that you know what to expect.

Ensure extra "conveniences" which will make the experience more fun, interesting and comfortable. These may be GPS, mobile map apps of the region, guides with information about local sights of interest, etc.

Use your strengths while traveling: You are a rather independent traveler - you can complete the trip even if others cancel on you. When preparing for a holiday with family and friends, you easily cope with details, such as technical preparation, equipment, electronic reservations, documents. We are not saying these tasks are necessarily the most pleasant ones, we are just saying that probably you're the person who will manage them the fastest and in best way possible.

You can also rely on your analytical skills as well as on your ability to gather information - it can be extremely valuable on the road.

Your strength is the ability to rediscover familiar, favorite places and regain your energy as you return to them!

What is the best way to approach this book?

This book can provide you with valuable experiences - it will allow you to explore yourself and also to create an environment for the inner "recharge" you sometimes need so badly. Just go through the ideas in it one by one and choose the ones you think you will enjoy most. Process them and give in to your natural talent for organizing and planning.

Probably this book will be a personal experience for you - if someone close to you is also interested, think about whether you are ready to give your book to them or buy them their own copy.

The Sociable Traveler

Communicating with people is one of the pleasures of traveling - you particularly enjoy unexpected encounters, accidental meetings and incredible coincidences. You try to feel the overall atmosphere of the places you visit. What you find genuinely exciting are the thoughts and emotions of the locals, the special things and events that take place there.

You are not afraid of surprises and you can manage sudden turn of events. Unexpected circumstances and situations often pop up in your travels, and it is definitely not unusual for you to finish the day at a place you didn't even know about in the morning.

Recipe: Your perfect trip

Take a group of friends with you. If you can't, get to know the people you meet on the road.

Find a contact person - when you go somewhere for the first time, it is always fun to have the contact information of someone who lives in the area.

Always have a charged cell phone with you in case you suddenly feel like sharing something with your friends.

Make sure you have enough essentials - water, food, money - these will help you cope in unexpected situations.

When you find yourself at a new place, ask the locals about any social events during your stay (festivals, carnivals, celebrations, etc.). Sometimes fortune introduces you to incredible people and events.

Use your strengths while traveling: There are moments, when plans fail and travelers find themselves in crisis (even absurd) situations on the road. This is the time when you are quite valuable. If you need to look for help, clarify the right direction or just to make friends with the locals for the sake of a peaceful party, you do so with ease (well, of course, something could go wrong, when you don't speak the language for example, but there is no record of that ever stopping you, right?). Demonstrating the initiative and effortless communication can be extremely useful for your own experience as well as that of your companions. Your natural spontaneity makes you a fun companion - when the rest of the group needs cheering up, something new and extraordinary, you are the one to do it, boldly with your unfailing knack for improvising.

You have the talent for connecting with new people and finding the charm in unknown cultures.

What is the best way to approach this book?

Open it only after you are already on the road. Choose random pages. Probably, the extraordinary and difficult challenges will bring you the greatest satisfaction. Freely express your natural creativity and you'll see you are able to make your own unique adventures.

You can also use the book as a source of ideas, when you have to prepare a romantic experience for your significant other or plan a surprise for friends. Predictable and strictly fixed adventures are not probably your style, so this book may prove to be a valuable adviser!

The Spontaneous Traveler

The feeling of independence and freedom is valuable for you on every journey. Your best adventures are measured in inner experiences and memories, not in the number of likes on social networks. You naturally seek the new and unknown, which makes you a truly spontaneous traveler. You don't need a plan or a guide to have fun. You feel great even in secluded places. You can devote your holiday entirely to extraordinary activities and hobbies, not being bothered whatsoever by the puzzled look on the faces of others. Your intuition and curiosity often take you to unexpected places and your courage helps you manage extreme situations.

Recipe: Your perfect trip?!

Sorry, but we are not giving you one. Simply because it won't work for you. Go ahead, throw your basics in your bag/suitcase and hit the road!

Use your strengths while traveling:
When unexpected events occur, you are probably the person who will remain calm and act appropriately. While traveling you'll do well at activities which require more independence and imagination (building an improvised shelter, cooking, repairing something). Without much fuss you get stuck into things that other people lack the bravery or talent to deal with. Perhaps managing technical devices is also something you are quite good at compared to most people.

Look for unfamiliar places and try new things - you are the person who can genuinely appreciate them!

What is the best way to approach this book?

Find yourself a piece of personal space and open the book on a random page. Your intuition and specific mood will show you best which challenges fit that particular moment of your life. If possible, dive into adventures alone (or with a true soulmate) and by no means let yourself be dragged into group activities, strict schedules and pre-arranged programs!

Keep the book 'within arm's reach' - so that you can use it anytime you feel like it.

Dear traveler,

We are not saying that in any situation people can use their strengths in the best way possible. Still, we think that with its general guidance, the provided typology of travelers is quite valuable and gives you a good idea of personal traits.

When you are about to set out on a journey with a group of people, you can use the test to try to get to know the strengths of your companions. They can take the test in advance so that you can allocate the tasks and roles according to everyone's individual talents and interests.

If you recognize yourself in the respective profile, share it with your friends - this will help them to understand you better and will make your future travels together more pleasant. It is also possible to find through this test unsuspected things you have in common and set the beginning of new shared travels.

We wish you a strong tailwind!

Start with challenge number one:

1.
What to do if you are bored or short of ideas?

It happens to everyone. You go to a new place full of interesting things and people and yet, right at that moment, you're just not feeling it... and you're bored.

What to do?

Stop. Take a deep breath. Take this book and open it on a random page. Complete the challenge there, or open on another random page until you find the challenge that fits your momentary mood.

At the end of the book, there is a game of chance to help you find new towns - toss a coin or put your finger anywhere on the page with your eyes closed. See what you land on and prepare for a discovery!

OUTDOOR CHALLENGES

2.
Jump into a warm, open-air mineral pool while it's snowing

There are plenty of warm, mineral pools in the open air around the world. However pleasant they may be in the summer, there is nothing like getting into one in the winter, when snowflakes are falling from the sky and you are soaking in warm, mineral water, not caring about tiny details like weather forecasts or an air temperature more suited to polar bears...

How to do it: Don't forget to take a towel to dry yourself off as quickly as possible as you climb out of the pool. Also take your favorite warm drink in a thermos for pure bliss (coffee, cappuccino, tea and rum, etc.).

A couple of ideas:

The Blue Lagoon in Iceland - The Blue Lagoon gets its name from the incredible color created by the mixture of fresh and salt water. It lies 40 km (24 miles) from the capital of Iceland - Reykjavík. The Blue Lagoon contains around 6 million liters (1.5 million gallons) of geothermal water, which renews itself naturally every 40 hours. The temperature is 37°C (98°F). Another cheaper and more tranquil option is the Myvatn Nature Baths nearby.

Japanese onsen - "onsen" is a type of spring that is very common in Japan. Visit Beppu, a city on the island of Kyushu, with its "Hells of Beppu" - geothermal hot spots, each differently colored due to the mineral content in the water.

3.

Night Challenge

There are many attractions which stay open even when it's dark outside. There are also events created to make your night more interesting. It's a different world when you trade the light of the sun for the light of the moon and the stars.

A couple of ideas for night events: European Night of Museums (every year on a Saturday, around 18th May - the International Day of Museums), European Literature Night (in May - celebrities read excerpts from European works of art - www.literaturenights.eu), European Theatre Night (in November - www.nocdivadel.cz/en). European Researchers' Night - research centers and museums open doors to show their achievements (every year in late September - ec.europa.eu/research/researchersnight/index_en.htm). Open-air cinema to enjoy a movie under the stars.

A couple of ideas for attractions open during the night: Every summer from May until October the Colosseum in **Rome**, Italy, is open until midnight on Mondays, Thursdays, Fridays and Saturdays (reservation necessary). In **New York** the Brooklyn Museum has free admission until 11 p.m. the first Saturday of each month (except September); the Top of the Rock observation deck at Rockefeller Center offers 70th floor views of Manhattan until midnight (last elevator up is at 11 p.m.), and the Empire State Building's observation deck is open until 2 a.m. In **Bangkok**, Thailand, every district has its own night market where you can find all kinds of food, goods and fun activities, at the same time immersing yourself the best way possible into local life. Try the biggest market, Rot Fai, or the bohemian JJ Green Night Market.

A couple of ideas for other night adventures:
Join a night sky watch through a telescope (find the

nearest astronomical observatory and check possible dates).

Organize a night picnic with lanterns/candles/ campfire, for example, combined with viewing the Perseid meteor shower (see Challenge 7) on the beach in mid-August.

For seasoned travelers: Take a **night walk** through the mountains. Under the only light of the moon or a headlamp - with an experienced guide or along trails you know like the back of your hand. Night walks are an experience that is hard to forget.

4.

Go out of range for 24 hours

You are constantly online. You follow the events on the social networks and sometimes it's as if the real world has disappeared. We challenge you to go for at least 24 hours to a place where electronic devices are out of range. We challenge you to feel that you are here and you are here now, instead of drifting through virtual space.

For seasoned travelers: Deliberately turn off all your devices for a day. Get out of range for a week.

5.
Bathe in a waterfall

Enjoy a free shower from nature. If you try to find pictures of the waterfalls listed below, without a shadow of a doubt you will want to shower there next time.

A couple of ideas: Skogafoss (Iceland), Havasu (Grand Canyon, USA), Ouzoud (Morocco), Skradinski buk (Croatia), Taranaki (New Zealand), Kempty (India). Or just visit the nearest waterfall to you.

6.
Celebrate the International Picnic Day

On International Picnic Day (every year on **18 June**), enjoy one of the best ways to be close to nature. The importance of picnics dates back to the Victorian Age when young men and women could spend time together in the open. Back in the day, they would bring fancy meals, sandwiches, sweets and crackers. Nowadays picnics require far less effort, but they can be a good reason finally to go somewhere you've been meaning to, but haven't had the chance.

How to make it more interesting: You can give the picnic a theme - everyone to wear red, to bring only Italian cuisine, tea and board games, a candlelit picnic, etc. To make it more fun, you can throw in a kite, slackline, hacky sack, badminton or a frisbee.

Fun fact... According to the Guinness Book of World Records, the biggest picnic in the world was organized in Lisbon, Portugal, on 20 June 2009 with more than 20 000 participants.

7.

See a shooting star and make a wish come true

Seeing a shooting star to make a wish may seem to you like pure chance. The truth is, you can help chance come your way by being in the right place at the right time. Every year, around 12 August, the sky night fills with hundreds of shooting stars (or meteorites to be exact). The reason is the annual meteor stream called Perseids.

Fun fact... The meteors are called Perseids because when we look at the sky it appears they come from the constellation Perseus. In Western European countries they are known as "the tears of Saint Lawrence" as the Perseids peak on the night of the Catholic holiday celebrating St.

Lawrence. In fact, the shooting stars we see in the sky are part of the comet Swift-Tuttle.

How to do it: The Perseids can be observed from late July until late August and they peak around 12 August (look up the date for the respective year). During the peak, hundreds of meteorites can be seen every hour. To make the most out of the experience, you need to go to a place where there is no artificial lighting (far from cities and villages) - you can combine it with a night picnic (see Challenge 3). You can see the Perseid meteor shower best in the Northern Hemisphere and down at the mid-southern latitudes.

A couple more ideas: There are other meteor streams throughout the year (Geminids in mid-December, Lyrids in mid-April, Quadrantids in late December - early January) when you can see a shooting star.

8.

Go kayaking (*or sailing*)

Discover new coastlines and reach places accessible only by boat. Take a camera (in a waterproof case) and photograph seahorses, birds, fish and other water-dwellers. Pack your lunch and go sailing for the whole day.

How to do it: The most common misconception is that you need to be able to swim to go kayaking. The authors of this book are living proof of just the opposite. You wear a life jacket and the tourist kayaks are much more stable than they appear at first glance. It is also appropriate for children. Kayaking in rivers and lakes is quite calm. The sea can be rough but you can participate in your own expedition finding secret bays and small islands where you can stop to eat and sunbathe.

9.

Go white water rafting

Let the rapids boost your adrenaline as your inflatable boat bounces up and down along the river. Swimming is not a necessary skill - as long as you're not afraid of water. Spring is the best time for rafting when rivers are high and the experience is more extreme.

A couple of ideas: In the USA go rafting along the Colorado River, in Europe - try the Tara River (Bosnia and Herzegovina). In Africa - go down the Zambezi in the company of hippos and crocodiles. The South American Futaleufú River in Chile offers an adrenaline boost amid the beautiful mountain landscapes of Patagonia, and Río Upano in Ecuador will take you on an adventure in the rainforest. The Coruh River in Anatolian Turkey is one of the fastest in the world.

10.

Go diving and discover sunken ships and underwater rock forests

If 71% of Earth's surface is covered with water and you can't dive, this means that even if you never stop going around the world by land, you don't stand a chance of knowing more than one-third of the planet. Discover a whole new world as you learn to dive - because in the blue deep, there aren't only fish and seaweed.

A couple of ideas: The world's top 10 diving destinations include Barracuda Point Malaysia, Palau (Micronesia), the Red Sea (Egypt), the Blue Hole in Belize, night diving into the bioluminescent waters near Hawaii, Bali, the Maldives, the Seychelles, and the Great Barrier Reef (Australia).

11.

See a shipwreck - without going underwater

It's human nature - we are drawn to tragedy and decay. We roam around abandoned villages, enter buildings carrying legends of ghosts and dive to reach sunken ships. If diving is not your passion, we challenge you to visit one of the most famous shipwrecks in the world... without having to dive.

A couple of ideas:

Zakynthos, Greece - At Navagio Beach, you will see the remains of a vessel washed ashore. You can take a peek from the high rocks or reach it by boat.

Muynak, Uzbekistan - Outside the town of Muynak (or Moynaq) in Uzbekistan, in the direction of the Aral Sea, you will witness a sinister view along the road - the skeletons of ships and fishing boats abandoned long ago in the desert. Up until about 30 years ago Muynak was a sea harbor but today it is in the middle of the desert, 50 km (30 miles) from the coast, after the rivers were diverted for irrigation purposes, and so the road leading to the Aral Sea turned into a ship graveyard.

Sydney, Australia - Homebush Bay in Sydney has become the final resting place of no longer operating ships. Some of them were swallowed by mangroves, growing over the rusty decks.

12.
Try a new outdoor sport

Talk to your friends about the things they've been doing

lately, search the Internet or try out something you've been meaning to for quite some time now.

A couple of ideas: Tai chi, yoga on the beach or the grass, rock climbing, mountain running, ski, snowboard, road or mountain cycling, surfing or windsurfing, diving - find your new favorite hobby, which will force you outside to spend more time in the fresh air. If it turns out to be your new passion, it will take you to newer and newer places to practice.

13.

Walk barefoot on grass or sand

When you find yourself on a meadow or a beach, take off your shoes and walk barefoot for a while. The morning dew on the grass adds to the great feeling and makes the experience even more special.

Why do it: Walking barefoot improves blood circulation, the position of the body slows down inflammatory processes in the body. According to some more spiritual beliefs, it connects you with Mother Earth and recharges your batteries.

14.
Hike in a mountain, climb a new peak

Go somewhere high and feel like a deity looking over their lands. If you have trouble finding your way, you don't know the trails or are worried you might get lost, join your mountaineering friends or sign up for a tourist club. If you are a keen hiker, your challenge is this: take a friend of yours who has never been that high before to one of your walks through the mountains.

How to do it: For a hike in the mountain you need several basic things - a comfortable backpack and shoes, a windproof jacket, a raincoat, tourist utensils and cutlery (plate, mug, fork and Swiss army knife), a mat, a headlamp/flashlight, water (sometimes you can't get it on the route), light and high-energy foods (nuts, dried fruit), a first-aid kit.

How to make it more interesting: Celebrate reaching the top with a bottle of champagne and share it with the other hikers. This is an achievement worthy of a proper celebration!

Get inspired...
Jack Kerouac said it best: "Because in the end, you won't remember the time you spent working in the office or mowing your lawn. Climb that goddamn mountain".

15.

Sleep in a tent and get your biological clock back to normal

Change the asphalt under your feet for grass or fine sand and (re)discover the joy of sleeping in fresh air, regardless of the time or day of the week, with your most serious responsibility for the day being to lie in the shade.

Why do it: Research shows that camping for a whole week reboots a person's biological clock. The modern way of life interferes with normal sleep because of the continuous exposure to artificial light and the body's decreased access to sunlight. All animal species on Earth have developed biological cycles connected to the sunrise and the sunset. Scientists have found that the widespread use of electric light after 1930 impacted on our internal physiological clocks, which allows us to stay awake till much later than evolution planned for. A group of volunteers in a research study at the University of Colorado Boulder were taken camping for a week, without being allowed to use flashlights or any electronic devices. At night the only light came from the campfire. As a result, the time the volunteers went to sleep and woke up synchronized with the sunrise and the sunset and for these seven days they managed to reboot their biological clocks.

How to make camping more interesting: Bring candles to create an even more memorable atmosphere (if there is wind and it blows them out, dig small holes in the sand/soil to put the candles in). Use a flashlight to make a theater of shadows.

For seasoned travelers:

Option 1: Spend the night under the stars in only a sleeping bag (especially appropriate for summer on the beach).

Option 2: Sleep in a tent on a weekday evening, then go to work on time the next day (see *Challenge 32*).

16.
Sweet camper van life

Having a camper van gives you the chance to choose your view during your morning coffee. You are independent and it almost feels like home. If the time to buy your first van hasn't come yet, hire one - for several days of happy traveling without schedules and plans.

For seasoned travelers: You've read all those travel blogs of people who left their jobs and embarked on a journey around the world by van. We'll say no more. You know what to do.

17.
Spend the afternoon in a hammock

Get a colorful hammock (it could be a pocket hammock, which is light and easy to carry). You may not believe it but for some people (let's say people with problems), spending an entire afternoon in a hammock while reading a book or simply listening to the birds and the wind is one of the biggest challenges in their lives. If you are one of these people, take this as a personal challenge.

For seasoned travelers: Spend summer nights in a hammock (in the woods, on the beach, in your own yard or even on the balcony - all these have been personally tested). Have in mind that you might need a mat or a thicker sleeping bag if you sleep in a hammock in the mountains (otherwise there will be lots of teeth chattering).

18.

Fly high: ride a zip line (*forest trolley*)

The wind in your hair and a 60 km/h (40 mph) flight are among the irreplaceable advantages of riding down a zip line. We have seen with our own eyes how people, claiming to be afraid of heights and certain that they would never make the descent down... line up for a third time.

A couple of ideas: Zip World Velocity in Wales, Great Britain is considered to be the fastest zip line - up to 160 km/h (100 mph), and the longest one is the Sasquatch in Whistler, Canada (more than 2 km/1.3 miles down).

19.
Cross 'via ferrata'

In Italian 'via ferrata' means "iron road". If you are afraid of heights, you will need nerves of iron to cross the rocky route but the best part is that you are secured the whole time and, in fact, finishing the route is completely safe. Today the system of ladders, metal ropes, suspension bridges and railings make the rock phenomena accessible not only to professional climbers. This adrenaline activity is something like an appetizer, which will build up your appetite and perhaps make you try out actual rock climbing.

A couple of ideas: World ratings for the most exciting via ferrata routes include destinations, such as Mount Kenya (the highest in the world, following a route along a dormant volcano); the Dolomites in Italy (those routes, unlike most, were built by the military during World War II in order to move swiftly and safely across the mountain); Mer de Glace (in Chamonix, Switzerland); Telluride (in San Juan Mountains, Colorado, USA); La Guagua (7 km/4.5 miles along a volcanic rock in Tamadaba Natural Park on Gran Canaria island, Spain).

20.
Go inside an extraordinary cave

Making caves accessible, very much like via ferrata, allows the ordinary, sneaker-wearing tourist to see some of the wonders of nature. Every cave hides some extraordinary secret to surprise you - be it glow-worms or underwater lakes.

A couple of ideas: Son Doong in Vietnam is the biggest cave in the world known today. In Batu Cave, Malaysia, the Hindus built cave temples. In Waitomo Cave, New Zealand, there are glow-worms - a magical sight in the complete darkness. Vatnajokull in Iceland is a cave located in a glacier. The Blue Grotto cave on Capri island looks as if it emits light.

21.
Bungee jump

It's not for everybody, but if you're wondering whether to do it, sign up, stand at the edge of the bridge and you will find out if you'll manage it.

The scariest places in the world to bungee jump:
Macau Tower in Macau, Asia, is the highest place to

bungee jump according to Guinness World Records - the site rises 233 m/ 764 feet above ground. You can also jump from a bridge over the Corinth Canal (it connects continental Greece with the Peloponnese Peninsula) - at a height of 79 m/ 259 feet. One of the most beautiful places to jump from is Victoria Falls (on the border of Zambia and Zimbabwe) - at a height of 111 m/ 364 feet.

22.

Paraglide or do a parachute jump

Not every human was born to be a bird but if you are still wondering if you got the wrong biological species - try. There's no other way to find out. Paraglider, hang glider, powered hang glider - these are meant for a free soar in the sky. Parachute jumping is for advanced sky explorers. Those who are very advanced just sign up for freefall or pilot courses.

How to do it (*if you want to but you're not brave enough*): Research shows that taking risks is contagious. In other words, if you are surrounded by adventurers, you are far more likely to get addicted to something you might think you're not brave enough to do.
Just fascinating, isn't it?

23.
Gather herbs and wild berries in summer

While taking walks through mountains and fields in the summer, gather some herbs, dry them and make yourself some homemade tea for the cold winter mornings. If you can't identify herbs, get a guide, download a mobile app which can tell them apart (there are a number of apps in different languages) or hire a guide (ask at the tourist centers of natural parks).

Also gather wild strawberries, raspberries, blackberries and blueberries in summer. If the harvest is abundant, you can make homemade jam. Put a label on each jar saying not only the type of berry but also the year and place they were gathered. Add funny notes. "Jam from wild raspberries picked in the Alps 2017, when Ann fell in the bushes and James fell too because he laughed so hard". And thus, from plain jam it becomes jam with a story.

24.
Feel like an ant among rock phenomena

Great poets have praised the might of nature for centuries, but this doesn't mean a thing until you find yourself in the

shadow of giant rock formations, steep rocky shores and...
you feel like a teeny-tiny ant.

A couple of ideas:

Cappadocia Chimneys - million of years ago, volcanoes
erupted in this part of Turkey and the wind and rain did
the rest as they shaped the lava into fairy rock chimneys.
While in Cappadocia, don't miss out on the rock-hewn
houses and churches, which are several centuries old.

Ha Long Bay, Vietnam - it's as if an ancient giant threw
rocks into the sea. Today, more than 1600 large and
small islands, most of which are uninhabited, create a
magical landscape for sailing.

Giant's Causeway, Northern Ireland - once again the
work of a giant - with his causeway of hexagonal basalt
columns, which helps him keep his feet dry from the sea.
An amazing experience for all non-giants.

Uluru (Ayers Rock), Australia - If there was only one
natural sight of interest in Australia that everybody
knew, it would be the famous rock that changes color
from violet to fiery red depending on the time of day
and the weather conditions. Here, the sense of your
own insignificance acquires enormous proportions - the
circumference of the base of Uluru being 9 km (5 miles),
to be exact.

25.

Sled down a slope as in your childhood years

Although this is considered to be entertainment for children, we know from experience that it's not so bad for adults either. Jumping into snowdrifts is fun no matter how old you are. If you still feel embarrassed, take some children with you - as a kind of 'cover-up'.

26.

Jump in the snow after taking a sauna in the name of health

"If sauna, liquor and tar don't help, your condition's fatal."
— Finnish saying.

Cooling down after a sauna is as important as heating up. It shouldn't happen too abruptly but if you go to Finland in the winter, you'll see people jumping into the ice-cold water of a lake or rolling in the snow after a sauna. Not that it's strictly considered normal, but it's not an uncommon sight, either. After this shock to your system, don't forget to pat yourself down with the birch twigs that can be found in every Finnish sauna. For health.

The Finnish have turned the healthy benefits of saunas into their religion and today almost all new apartments have a separate space for the sauna next to the bathroom.

27.

Go snowshoeing in the mountains

You don't even have to be an experienced mountaineer or possess snowshoes. You can hire snowshoes, sticks and a guide and enjoy a new interpretation of the word "silence" in the winter mountains. Hikes take from several hours to several days.

Why do it: Because the snowshoes can take you to places in the mountains you can't reach any other way. You will find yourself in places where no tourist has set foot for weeks. You will feel the cold, whiteness and closeness to nature in a perfectly new way.

28.

Go for an adventure (*you don't have to be Bear Grylls*)

"The adventures first," said the Gryphon in an impatient tone: "explanations take such a dreadful time."
(from "Alice in Wonderland")

If you don't have the time, money or courage to become a discoverer or adventurer who roams the planet in risky expeditions, this doesn't mean that you can't have adventures in your life. Create your own mini-adventures to awaken your inventive spirit.

How to do it: Adventure is a broad term, which carries a different meaning for everyone. An adventure is something that you don't usually do. Something that makes you enthusiastic, excited and maybe a little nervous. Which adventure have you always dreamed of? Realize a mini version of it first. Put up a tent in the back yard or in the living room (with the help of the children and the dog). Go on a one-day expedition into the woods and imagine that you are on a lonely island and you need to find food in the wilderness. Your adventure - your ideas.

Get inspired... Alastair Humphreys is a true adventurer, who crossed the Atlantic Ocean in a kayak, traveled the world by bike and has been on several Arctic expeditions. He pays special attention to what he calls

"microadventures" - small steps for those who do not believe in their potential for adventure, but carry enough positive energy and adventurous spirit.
Read more on
www.alastairhumphreys.com/microadventures-3

29.

Learn to make fire without matches or lighters

In a world of modern conveniences and lighters, there is nothing more exciting than creating something our ancestors had to learn how to do, like starting a fire.

How to do it: The friction-based method with dry sticks is quite famous, but it will make you sweat. Here is an easier option. Take a round plastic bottle, reading glasses or fill a plastic bag with water and close it tight. All of these objects could be used to concentrate sunlight onto a black part of a newspaper (smoke appears right away) or onto gathered kindling (dry grass, pine needles, dry moss, etc.). Once the kindling is burning, put it in the base of the already prepared pile of wood.

30.

Learn to use the sun as a sole guiding point

Using the sun as a guiding point may save your life in the wilderness, backwoods, the Sahara or any other place where you find youself with no compass or guiding point. It's also an essential skill if your compass fails you. Above all, this will allow you to brag about your incredible skills - worthy of a whole Survivor season - to friends and strangers.

How to do it:

Ingredients: sun, long straight object (a stick)
Time: 15-20 minutes
Execution: Take a long straight object - a stick is best, ski stick or whatever straight object you have at hand in the above-mentioned wilderness, where you might not have much of a choice. In the worst case scenario, you could play the "straight object" but we doubt you would be willing to stand still for 20 minutes under the sun. Put the object into the ground at an angle of 90 degrees (it is important for the angle to be as close to 90 degrees as possible) and mark with a pebble or twig the end of the object's shadow. Wait for 15-20 minutes. In that time the shadow will move. Take another pebble and mark the new end of the shadow. Draw a straight line between the start and end point of the shadow (the two pebbles). This line points east-west, the first point is west and the second - east.

31.

Ride a bike slowly between villages (*and other bike challenges*)

With a smile on your face, cross villages and talk to locals about this year's harvest of apples and how much the piglets cost. We bet you have no idea. Have a beer with one of those locals who spends the day scanning passers-by in a cafe in the center.

A couple of ideas: We could write a separate book on challenges for cyclists, but let's start with a few:

1. Instead of village roads, explore dirt roads.

2. Try to bike as far as you can for a day.

3. Try mountain biking (which from a smooth descent may turn into an adrenaline experience).

4. Sign up for a bike club.

5. Join a cycling group or tour, organized near you.

Get inspired... L'Eroica vintage bike ride in Tuscany, Italy. Every year thousands of cyclists put on vintage leather pants, hop on their vintage bikes, don a fine ancient cap and embark on a journey into the past. L'Eroica vintage bike ride is one of the most exciting ways to get to know Tuscany on two wheels. The event aims to preserve the sport's romantic beauty of the past, without a competitive aspect. That is why, if you want to participate, you must do it with a vintage road bike made before 1987 and nothing else. There are routes of 38 km (23 miles), 75 (46 miles), 135 km (83 miles) or 209 km (129 miles). Both the starting and final points of all routes is the town of Gaiole in Chianti, about 65 km (40 miles) from Florence.

32.

Sleep in the wild on a weekday (*without taking a day off*)

Sleeping under the stars is the best way to get new energy and ideas for work. You can do it after you finish work and go back to the office the next day on time. If you find the idea adventurous and absurd - it's only because not everybody does it. But we guarantee you will have broad grin spread across your face the next morning. Tested by the authors of this book.

How to do it: In a few easy steps (try with the closest mountain, hill, camping site or wild locations around you):

1. After work on a summer Tuesday take the bus to the the closest wild place where you can put up a tent. If

there is no public transport, go by car or by bike.

2. Set up the tent before dusk.

3. For a boost of courage and to keep bears at bay, take a vodka/whisky shot or whatever medicine you have against bears.

4. Start a fire and grill some sausages.

5. [Optional] Some locals from the near village come to visit, you have a drink together and they leave, and you go to sleep in you bed under the stars.

6. Get up at 7 am, have breakfast and pack your stuff. If you have a Sherpa around, you give them your bags. If not, you carry them yourself, awaiting better times.

7. Take the bus back to the city and take a quick shower.

8. You enter the office on time, a broad grin on your face.

Everything works out perfectly, especially if you happen to have a shower at your workplace.

33.

Hug a very special tree

...and get fresh energy from nature. If you want to hug a truly special or unique tree, you can do it while traveling.

A couple of ideas: Dragon trees on the island of Socotra, Yemen - those amazing plants that make the island look as if it's a land from another planet. The Avenue of the Baobabs on the island of Madagascar is probably the most photographed street there (without even being a real street!). It won't be so easy, however, to hug the largest living tree on the planet - the giant sequoia General Sherman (with a height of 84 m/275 ft) because its circumference at ground is 31 m/102 ft. The tree is located in Sequoia National Park, California, USA. One more idea. In many cultures, trees are a symbol of family and kinship. Get together the whole family and plant a tree in a place where you all love going to. Then you'll have occasion to go there even more often.

34.

When you are on a holiday, get up early and see the sunrise at least once

Or don't go to bed at all and watch the sunrise - a good enough option for those who can't get up early.

Get inspired... by Robert M. Pirsig and his book "Zen and the Art of Motorcycle Maintenance": "I started to roll over for more sleep but heard a rooster crowing and then became aware we are on vacation and there is no point in sleeping."

A couple more ideas: Watch the sunrise on top of a hill. From the beach. From the camping site - as you lie inside an unzipped tent. From a boat - because you've gone for a row in the dark. In a flower field (for example lavender fields in blossom). From your window - get up specially for the sunrise and then go back to sleep. From the car - because you have just arrived after driving all night.

35.

Challenge with a bench for every season

Choose a favorite bench at a beautiful place that fills you with energy (it could be in the mountain, in the park, in a favorite town). Sit on it every season. Take four photos at a different time of the year and make a collage of them. Notice how everything around you changes and how you have changed.

Get inspired... a Chinese proverb: "If you stay long enough in one place the whole world passes you by."

36.

Organize a treasure hunt

This game, originally for children, creates the same enthusiasm among adults. You can play it on the beach, in the mountains, in the city and even in your neighborhood. How to do it: Make a list of the things that participants need to find and bring back (or photograph). Everybody receives the same list, whoever collects all treasures first wins. If you are in the mountain, this could be a cone, a red flower, round pebble, animal-shaped rock, etc. On the beach - clam, shell, etc.

37.

Hunt treasures with Geocaching

'Geocaching' is a contemporary form of treasure hunt. You need a smartphone or GPS to play. People from all over the world hide various objects in the most incredible places in different countries, which you need to find as you follow the coordinates. When you find the treasure, you have to replace it with another item - and the game continues for the next player who will visit the location.
More on www.geocaching.com

38.

Discover an abandoned place and take a walk in the past

Abandoned places are interesting, sad and scary all at the same time as they have the most exciting stories to tell. If you end up in an abandoned place, take a peek inside. A house, monument, a whole village... You may discover an object, as if just left there by its owners - you will get an insight into the past life of the place and the people, who used to dream, work and rest here...

How to do it: There are groups on social networks, where you can find ideas and inspiration for abandoned places with truly impressive stories. There are websites dedicated to urbex (urban exploration), where you can see pictures and read stories, even if you have no intention of becoming an abandoned places discoverer. Always take with you shoes with solid soles (you never know in what condition you'll find the place), a flashlight and a camera to photograph your findings for all eternity.

39.
Practice Gokotta

"Gokotta" (from Swedish - Gökotta) is an untranslatable word, meaning "to rise at dawn in order to go out and listen the birds sing"

Getting up early on weekends is not a common practice, which is why we challenge you to do exactly that in the spirit of Swedish gokotta. Wake up before the birds to hear them sing in the morning and welcome the sun.

For seasoned travelers: Instead of getting up early on a weekend, have a fresh start of your working day with a song from nature, leaving all your colleagues wondering where your good mood comes from.

Tradition's origin?

In some parts of Sweden there is a tradition of going out in nature on Ascension Day (40 days after Easter) to listen to the birds, especially the cuckoo, sing their songs for the first time in spring. Even churches in many parts of the country agree to hold the service on Ascension morning in the open so that believers could hear the cuckoo sing - a symbol of spring.

40.
Celebrate the day of the summer solstice

In many parts of the world the day of the summer solstice (21 June) is special. Besides being the longest day of the year (in the northern hemisphere), this is also the day which marks the link between people, the Earth and the Sun, and is celebrated with dances, bonfire, making wreaths, gathering healing plants and herbs, performing magic and mystical rituals.

How to do it:

Go to the mountain/forest/park/beach - go for a walk and/or take photos

Watch the sunrise on the longest day of the year

Gather herbs

Discover or think of your own sun ritual

A couple of ideas: about special places in the world to go to on the day of summer solstice:

1. Stonehenge – this is one of the places where the largest number of sun worshippers gather from all over the world.

2. Sweden – the Swedish express their joy by dancing around a high stake, adorned with flowers. They make wreaths, which the girls wear on their heads.

3. Denmark – In the whole of Scandinavia there is a tradition of making a huge bonfire during the night of the summer solstice. The Danish go to extremes as they burn up scarecrows.

4. Finland - in Helsinki, they celebrate the night of the summer solstice with a loud street festival, and the day is known as Juhannus - or St. John's Day.

One more idea: Get dressed and watch the sunrise on the day of the Winter Solstice (between 21 and 23 December in the northern hemisphere).

41.
Spend at least an hour every weekend close to nature

Spend at least an hour close to nature every weekend for a year. Find the time to go out of the urban matrix between your other responsibilities. It would be best to choose a place with no human interference with nature (a forest, meadow, wild beach, etc.).

How to do it: Every week, take a picture of the time you spend in nature to remember your mood. Collect all pictures in an album, numbered "week 1", "week 2". You can add a story about where you've been and how you felt (keep it in a scrapbook or online in a file/blog).

ONCE-IN-A-LIFETIME CHALLENGES

Travels, adventures and emotions to experience at least once in your lifetime. Go through our ideas and jot down your own dreams. Then dare to make them come true.

42.

Make your biggest travel wish come true

The first and most fundamental obstacle to making your dreams come true is... that you often think it's not possible. Say your biggest travel dream is to see a polar bear, swim with sharks, see the Northern Lights or backpack around the world. Piece of cake.
Read below carefully:

Write down your biggest travel dream:

. . . .
. . . .

A plan for making big travel dreams come true:

1. You need a plan. Write down what you want, find out how much it would cost and what else needs to be done (for instance, learn to swim).

. . . .
. . . .

2. If your dream requires more funds, open a separate bank account (the money in the general account often pays other expenses - you need a separate account, from which it is difficult to withdraw). You can use the coin technique (see Challenge 99), or ask your friends and relatives to give you money for your dream instead of gifts on holidays. Think about your expenses. Is there anything that you actually don't need but still spend money on? You could sell some of your stuff you haven't used for years.

3. If your dream requires serious effort on your part (for example, you want to climb Mount Everest or cycle thousands of kilometers), make a training plan and start right away.

4. Try to set a realistic deadline. It's easier to pursue a goal if it is fixed at a point in the future.

5. Tell all your friends about your dream and the efforts you put in. Their support will help you not to give up.

6. You're all set!

Get inspired...

There are thousands of blogs by people all over the world who have made their biggest travel dream come true. So can you. Seek inspiration in your favorite travel blog.

43.

Get close to an animal in its natural habitat

Our lives are so dominated by concrete and steel that an encounter with an animal in the wild is a rare and exciting experience (unlikely it was like that for our cave ancestors). This challenge will push you to discover the natural habitats of your favorite animals and find a way to arrange a meeting with them.

A couple of ideas:

Face to face with polar bears in Canada - They say that in the Canadian town of Churchill there are more bears than residents. In the fall, the polar bears migrate close to the city to wait for the Hudson river to freeze over. At that time, hundreds of tourists get on the specially designed "tundra buggies" and dive into ecotourism and close encounters with polar bears. There is also a "polar bear prison" in the town, where the local authorities keep the bears who attack the town and let them free when the bay freezes.

Dive into the Great Barrier Reef - Diving into 2000 km (1240 miles) of colorful corals and brightly-colored fish near the Australian coast is like being in a magical world.

Go on a safari in Africa - Experience a close encounter with the animals you've seen only on TV in the national parks of Kenya, South Africa and Tanzania.

Whale watching - Among the most popular places in the world for whale watching are Vancouver Island and the Gulf of Saint Lawrence (Quebec, Canada), Boston (USA), Husavik and Reykjavik (Iceland), Scotland and the Azores.

203 Travel Challenges

Write here which animals you'd love to see and where you dream of seeing them:

. . . .
. . . .
. . . .

44.

Run a (*crazy*) marathon

There are marathons you run simply to prove to yourself that you can do it. Start with them. There are those that are a really special experience.

A couple of ideas:

Every big city organizes a marathon at least once a year. Below you will find a list of some of the most extreme, fun and emblematic marathons around the world:

Great Wall Marathon - 42 km (26 miles) along the Great Wall of China

Antarctica Marathon and Half - Where else can you run among seals, penguins, whales and icebergs?

Marathon Des Sables in the Sahara Desert - When you say Sahara Desert, a marathon of 251 km (155 miles) is hardly the first thing that comes to mind. On top of that, marathoners not only sign up for the event but also have to run the distance of six regular marathons in six consecutive days.

The Maldon Mud Race in UK - Few marathon runners around the world boast the enthusiasm of those who take part in the Maldon Mud Race, along with the enormous amount of mud they get covered in. The race through the natural mud, which could easily be defined as a 'swamp', requires nerves of steel to complete the route of 400 m (1310 ft) - running, falling, getting up and even crawling.

Lake Baikal Ice Marathon, Russia - The extreme race is the regular distance of slightly more than 42 km (26 mi) but along the frozen surface of Lake Baikal, in conditions that only Siberia, Russia can offer in early March.

Santa Speedo Run, Boston, USA - To run the annual Santa Speedo Run in Boston you need a Speedo-like bathing suit, holiday colors are preferred. You will also need some Christmas flair (Santa hat, beard, Christmas socks, etc.). December weather in Boston is far from the temperature suitable for bathing suits. So the runners are allowed (recommended even) to have a drink or two before the run.

For seasoned travelers: Run a mountain race.

45.

Have a beer at Oktoberfest (*and other famous beer destinations*)

In 1977 American Steven Petrosino drank 1 liter (33 ounces) of beer in the staggering 1.3 seconds, officially enshrined as a Guinness world record. Even if you're not so quick at finishing pints of beer, you wouldn't say no to tasting beer at some of the most emblematic places in the world - it is a challenge to be at one of them with a cold beer in your hand at least once in your lifetime.

A couple of ideas:

Oktoberfest in Munich and throughout Germany - Every year Munich is flooded with more than 6 million people from all over the planet, sometimes crossing tens of thousands of kilometers and flying over oceans and continents. There must be something about Oktoberfest! Indeed there is - beer, sausages and an excessive amount of skinny men's leather pants. Join the celebrations of King Ludwig I and Princess Therese's wedding anniversary. When they got married in 1810, Ludwig gave a sumptuous feast for Munich residents in honor of his wedding at Theresienwiese (or "Theresa's Meadow, derived from the name of the Princess). To learn more about the festival, visit oktoberfest.de.

Prague, Czech Republic - Beer is good and cheap, there are plenty of bars that offer beer, their own production.

London, UK - A number of local, import and craft beers (microbreweries with a bar everywhere you turn).

Ireland - In an Irish pub, you really are required to taste every beer wonder not yet part of your collection of world beers.

Belgium - Here beer is of such great variety that one liver won't be enough to take it all in. It's a heaven for fruit, chocolate and craft beer.

46.

Have a bottle of local wine with a view

"Years, lovers and glasses of wine; these things must not be counted"

Find out the local grape variety of the place you're going to and buy a bottle. Find some place with a view (of the sea, mountain tops, over a small town), sit down for a while and share the bottle with a loved one. No hurrying, no talking required. Picture the grape ripening in these lands under the same sun. Close your eyes and feel the aroma of wine.

How to really sense the aroma of wine? Close your

eyes and hold your nose. Have a sip of wine and keep it in your mouth. Your taste buds will sense some of the wine aroma. Then release your nose and you will feel the taste explode in your senses.

How do you know how old the wine is? Red wine: tilt the glass against a white napkin or something white and see the color of wine around the edge - if it is rather purple - the wine is young; if it is rather brick red - it's older. White wine - greenish hues means young wine, orange - mature wine.

Get inspired... by the Venetians. They call their wine... "shadow" or "shade" ("ombra" in Italian). The Venetian word for wine dates back to the old days when, legend has it, wine merchants at Piazza San Marco would move their wares throughout the day to stay out of the sun, in the shadow of the bell tower. And so the phrase "grab some shade" came to mean "grab a glass of wine". Venetians know this stuff. Look for your own wine shade.

A couple of ideas for local wine in...

Italy: When in Rome, look for the Cesanese and Aleatico wine grape varieties, in Venice ask for Prosecco and Amarone wines, in Tuscany - Chianto Classico and Brunello di Montalcino - best in a vineyard winery.

Spain: If you have already tried sangria, we challenge you to go deeper into the flowing sea of wine in Spain. If you are a fan of red wine, try the Tempranillo, Garnacha, Graziano, Monastrell, Mazuelo wine grape varieties. If you prefer white wine, look for Viura, Malvasia, Verdejo wine varieties. In Catalonia, make sure you try Cava - a sparkling wine, produced in the champagne method. In Andalusia, drink Sherry - a fortified wine (in this case brandy is added). In the Basque Country, try the fresh white wine with low alcohol content - Txakoli.

France: Beaujolais, Bordeaux (red and white), champagne, wines from the valleys of the Rhone and Loire rivers, Sancerre, wines from the Provence Region, Burgundy (red and white), Chablis. Whether it's in a glass, on tap or in a bottle from the wine list, you can rest assured that everything is carefully selected as the French take their wine very seriously. The rest is easy. Enjoy the joie de vivre ("the joy of living" in French), which in France is served in a wine glass.

47.
Drink whisky where it is created

Whisky is a religion with its cults and rituals. If you also pray to this particular God, here are some of the legendary whisky destinations around the world.

A couple of ideas:

The Old Bushmills Distillery, Ireland - the world's

oldest licensed distillery, and the only one which introduces visitors to a real ghost as they taste the drinks.

Jameson Distillery, Ireland - John Jameson is an Irish legend and if you happen to be passing through Dublin, stop by to hear the magical stories about alcohol vapor.

The Malt Whisky Trail in Scotland - the tremendous party swinging along the river Spey coast is beyond your imagination, considering that more than half of the distilleries in Scotland are there - from Glenfiddich to Glenlivet and Strathisla. The most remarkable is Cardhu, where Johnnie Walker's secrets are kept.

Bladnoch Whiskey Academy, Scotland - A small house in Bladnoch, just a bit beyond the end of the world, offers to introduce you to the production of whisky in the best way possible - by signing up for a three-day course of distilling and getting drunk, after which you most probably won't want (or won't be able) to leave.

Bar Hemingway at the Ritz Paris - As one of the most famous drinkers in the history of literature, Hemingway deserves to have a bar named after him. The Ritz Hotel honors posthumously its regular visitor by naming its bar Hemingway. If you want to be part of your own "Midnight in Paris", surrounded by Hemingway's photographs - stop by for a drink at the bar.

Jack Daniel's, USA - Lynchburg, Tennessee is a legendary place to take a good walk while listening to stories about Jack and where, without any judgement whatsoever, you could share your very own personal encounters with him. Curiously enough, Lynchburg's home county has been a dry county ever since the Prohibition in the United States. So if you want to enjoy your drink, you will have to go to the neighboring county.

48.

Dance at the Rio Carnival (*or another emblematic place*)

Dance the streets with the locals, visit the clubs in those places of the world, where dancing was born or it is more important than religion.

A couple of ideas: Join the samba street madness at the Carnival in Rio de Janeiro, Brazil. Try a tango in the streets of Buenos Aires, Argentina, or sirtaki in a Greek tavern. Why not flamenco in Spain, or salsa in the clubs in Cuba?

Write here where and what you would like to dance:
. . . .

49.

Travel around Spain like Don Quixote (*and other famous combinations of places&books*)

Before going to a country or town, read a story that takes place there. You could take the book with you (or upload it to your e-reader) and read it as you travel (perfect for long hours on a train or bus or during long stops).

A couple of ideas:

Japan: "Memoirs of a Geisha" by Arthur Golden, "Shōgun" by James Clavell or Haruki Murakami's novels.

India: "Passion India" and "El sari rojo" by Javier Moro, "Sorcerer's Apprentice" by Tahir Shah.

Amsterdam, the Netherlands: - "The Diary of Anne Frank" and then visit Anne Frank's real house at 263-267 Prinsengracht

Morocco: "In Arabian Nights: A Caravan of Moroccan Dreams" by Tahir Shah

Great Britain: - "Notes from a Small Island" and "The Road to Little Dribbling" by Bill Bryson, "You Are Awful (But I Like You)" by Tim Moore

Spain: "The Sun Also Rises" and "For Whom the Bell Tolls" by Ernest Hemingway, Federico García Lorca's poetry and plays, "Don Quixote" by Miguel de Cervantes.

Italy: Frances Mayes' books about Tuscany, "A Field Guide to the Italian Mind" by Beppe Severgnini, "Angels & Demons" by Dan Brown.

Greece: Gerald Durrell's Corfu Trilogy "My Family and Other Animals", "Birds, Beasts, and Relatives", "The Garden of the Gods".

France: Peter Mayle's books about Provence, "The Hunchback of Notre-Dame" by Victor Hugo

Books to read on the road: "On the Road" by Jack Kerouac, "Into the Wild" by Jon Krakauer, "The Great Railway Bazaar" by Paul Theroux, "The Geography of Bliss" by Eric Weiner, "The Innocents Abroad" by Mark Twain.

Your favourite books that you want to read as you travel but still haven't:

. . . .
. . . .
. . . .

50.
Visit your favorite celebrity's favorite places

Writers have their imaginary literary worlds, but they also have their real, authentic lives, which are just as worthy of being traced and re-lived. The same goes for musicians, actors, painters, scientists... Pick one of your favorite writers, musicians, actors whose footsteps you would like to follow in, and hit the road.

A couple of ideas:

Follow in Hemingway's footsteps in Cuba: Hemingway is everywhere in Havana and in different shapes - primarily alcoholic. If you were Hemingway and you announced where to find the best daiquiri in Havana (El Floridita bar) and the best mojito (La Bodeguita del Medio bar) - both still open today, years later worshippers would come in their hordes, following in your footsteps.

So you pictured it - and now you are the reborn Hemingway. Do you follow? Then the next stop in Havana is Ambos Mundos hotel where the writer lived for seven years in the 1930s. Room 501 is now a mini museum which you can visit during the day (we know you're the reborn Hemingway but they still won't let you sleep there). You will find the room as if the writer had just left in a hurry. Also open to visitors is Hemingway's house Finca Vigía in the small working-class town of San Francisco de Paula. Today the house is open to visitors (NB! It is, however, often closed suddenly for restorations) - every day between 10 am and 4 pm, on Sundays between 9 am and 1 pm.

Follow in Gabriel García Márquez's footsteps in Colombia: "One Hundred Years of Solitude" was published in 1967 and it gradually became one of the leading novels of 20th century as well as a fine example of the magic realism style. It tells the story of the Buendia family, whose patriarch is also a founder of Macondo. It is believed that Marquez portrayed Macondo drawing inspiration from his home place of Aracataca in Colombia. The weather in the river town is hot and people mostly grow bananas. Magic lurks around the dusty corners, or at least that's how the writer felt it. Today his home and the church he was baptized in are major tourist attractions, and Aracataca still keeps the spirit of the novel.

More: At 251 Menlove Avenue in Liverpool, you will find the house where John Lennon grew up. In Mexico City, at 247 Londres is the famous blue house of Frida Kahlo. In Montreux, not far from Freddie Mercury's home and studio, is his three-meter-tall statue, looking over Lake Geneva...

Write here celebrity-related destinations, where you would like to end up:

· ·
· ·
· ·

51.
Travel like in a movie

Shot after shot, you film your journey through real movie locations. In addition to retracing the steps of your favorite movie characters, you can film the familiar places and then make a video of your personal "movie" in a simple, easy-to-use video editor. For an extra special mood, play the soundtrack of a favorite movie as you travel.

A couple of ideas:

"The Fabulous Life of Amélie Poulain" - Go to Montmartre in Paris, once the kingdom of artists and quadrille dancers, now the kingdom of Amélie Poulain. Most of the movie's scenes were shot in this arrondissement. It would be best to take Lepic Street and look for number 15 where you will find Cafe des Deux Moulins (the Two Mills). True, Audrey Tautou won't serve you, but the atmosphere, up to the last movie poster, is the same as in the cafe in the movie.

"Star Wars": The fans of George Lucas's iconic series will remember that the home of young Luke Skywalker in the first parts of the saga is on a desert planet. This place really exists - on the planet Earth at that. It is a hotel in the small Berber town of Matmata in southern Tunisia. Its residents have lived in big, underground hollows for centuries. They dig through the walls to make rooms with tunnels serving as corridors.

"The Godfather" - The locations of Francis Ford Coppola's trilogy are numerous. One of them is the Italian village of Savoca in the Province of Messina, Sicily - the fictional home town of Vito Corleone. The scenes at Bar Vitelli (still in existence today) and Michael Corleone's wedding were also filmed there.

Write here a movie location you would like to visit:

. . . .
. . . .

52.
Feel like an ancient king or pharaoh

Ok, because of some weird misunderstanding, you weren't born with a silver spoon in your mouth. This, however, shouldn't stop you from feeling like a ruler - regardless of whether you prefer the strict Norwegians or the more free-spirited residents of Tonga to be your subjects. When you head for a walk through your lands, don't forget your crown and sceptre so that people can recognize you easily.

A couple of ideas:

The Pyramids of Giza - At the Great Pyramid of Giza near Cairo you can feel like the Egyptian Pharaoh Khufu. The Pyramid is about 140 m (460 ft) tall (it used to be taller but with erosion, it lost about 10 meters (33 ft) since its construction). The original casing stones were made of highly polished white limestone to tell from afar that here rests an important person. Check also the condition of the Sphinx - the guardian of the tombs. While in Egypt, go to the Valley of the Kings - the Egyptian kings' burial ground. However, keep in mind the Curse of the Pharaohs (don't open any ancient tombs!).

The Terracotta Army and the first Chinese emperor - The first Chinese emperor Qin Shi Huang wasn't very democratic, he burnt thousands of books and buried people alive. However, he had the fixed idea, which came to him at the age of 13, of building a huge tomb. The emperor was afraid of death and throughout his whole life he would seek from sorcerers the secret of immortality. Obviously, he didn't succeed, but his Mausoleum near Xian was found in 1974. Inside he is guarded by the famous terracotta army.

Taj Mahal - when you are in an exquisite ivory-white marble mausoleum, which looks more like a castle, you know that kings can love too. Shah Jahan built the Taj Mahal out of grief for his beloved Mumtaz, who died in childbirth. Today the place breaks all records in marriage proposals and the waiting time to take a photo.

53.
Feel like Mowgli in the jungle

"It is the hardest thing in the world to frighten a mongoose, because he is eaten up from nose to tail with curiosity. The motto of all the mongoose family is „Run and find out," and Rikki-tikki was a true mongoose."
—*"The Jungle Book" by Rudyard Kipling.*

Don't worry, we already know. We know you are just like the mongoose. A traveler's curiosity always takes them to places not visited before - the jungle, for example. It's where you can go trekking as well as a thousand other things.

A couple of ideas:

Fish for piranhas in the Amazon River - cast a fishing rod in the muddy water of the Brazilian Amazon and catch a predatory dinner.

Discover Khao Sok National Park in Thailand with the elephants - more and more tourists choose to be ethical and instead of riding elephants in the jungle, they discover it together with the elephants, both feet on the ground. Close to the park there are also houses on trees, bungalows and stilt houses, where you can spend the night.

Meet mountain gorillas at Volcanoes National Park, Rwanda - before making an appointment with the gorillas and meeting some of the best gorilla guides, watch the movie "Gorillas in the Mist".

54.

Discover your wettest self in one of the biggest aquaparks in the world

A waterproof phone case and a raw egg in the morning - they say it's good for the vocal cords and you will need your voice to scream your lungs out as you go down the waterslides and other attractions created by aquapark designers all around the world.

You can create your personal Top 20 Best Aquaparks In The World.

55.

Walk on water and in the clouds at the same time

Salar de Uyuni in Bolivia is one of the most emblematic places that inspires people to travel thousands of kilometers just for a photo. Ok, fine, hundreds of photos. It is the world's biggest salt flat. When it rains, a thin layer of water covers the flat and turns it into a huge mirror, reflecting the sky. This makes it possible to walk on water and in the clouds (their reflection) at the same time. An out-of-this-world experience!

Tip: When visiting Salar de Uyuni, remember to take your sunglasses and hat with you. As the amount of reflected light is very high, they will protect you from heavy sunburn.

56.

Test drive your favorite car make

Big car producers offer test drives of their new models. So even if you can't afford a new Ferrari right now, you can at least get a taste of the speed, glued to the seat.

57.

Go on a cruise

Cruises are not for everyone (like almost everything in this world, in fact). They are an excellent choice if you need a calmer holiday, if contemplating the sea helps you relax, if stopping for a day or two at different places is the change of scenery you need. Your cruise could be different - a party cruise, erotic cruise, round-the-world cruise (you will need more time for this one), river cruise, Antarctica cruise, adventure cruise...

58.

Go to a sculpture park... underwater

Telling someone you will spend part of your next holiday in the company of sculptures won't impress them much. If, however, after a few seconds of silence you add... "underwater". Bam!

A couple of ideas:

Molinere Underwater Sculpture Park, Grenada - in the Caribbean sea off the west coast of Grenada, West Indies. It was created by British sculptor Jason deCaires Taylor with the idea of engaging locals and increasing awareness of the surrounding environment.

Archaeological Park of Baiae, Naples, Italy - Once the ancient Romans' Las Vegas, today an ancient town below sea level. Baiae is one of the few underwater archaeological sculpture parks which are several centuries old. To see the town's remains you can either dive, or take a boat with a glass bottom.

Cancun Marine Park, Mexico - a coral reef and more than 470 sculptures by Jason deCaires Taylor.

Underwater Museum, Lanzarote - Europe's only underwater sculpture museum with sculptures by Jason deCaires Taylor.

59.

Go where 90% of animals and plants are unique to the planet

A long time ago Madagascar moved away from its surrounding continents and decided to start a new life on its own. It did just that. Today some scientists call it the Eighth Continent because almost 90% of animals and plants are endemic (they can be found only here and nowhere else on Earth). Look for lemurs, many types of chameleons (including the smallest known to zoologists) and walk along the Avenue of the Baobabs.

60.

While abroad, go to the hairdresser's/barber's

Here the challenge is not to go to the hairdresser's per se, but to do something abroad that you usually only do at home and perceive as a trivial activity - a haircut, manicure, or in Arab countries men can go to the barber's...

61.

Ice skate on some of the most beautiful ice rinks

Prepare the skates and show us a double axel (or triple fall on the ice - it depends on your level) on some of the most impressive ice rinks around the world.

A couple of ideas: Every winter (January - March) you can skate on Vienna Ice Dream in front of the City Hall. Nathan Phillips Square in Toronto, Canada, is also situated in front of the City Hall and will offer a memorable skating. One of the world's most famous ice rinks is the one in front of Rockefeller Center in New York, USA. The highest ice rink in the world was opened in Moscow - 354 m (1160 ft) high, sitting on the rooftop of the Eye skyscraper.

62.

Get lost in a magic garden

Not every garden in the world is just well-shaped bushes + fountains + benches. Sometimes gardens keep interesting stories and wonders and provide inspiration for the paintings of famous artists.

A couple of ideas:

Keukenhof, Holland - seven million flowers, hand-planted every year. There are more than 100 variaties of tulips alone. Almost one million people a year visit the park. It is located not far from Amsterdam, near the town of Lisse. Open only March - May.

The Garden of Cosmic Speculation in Scotland - If Alice's Wonderland did exist, then it would certainly be in Dumfries, Scotland under the name of the Garden of Cosmic Speculation. Inspired by science and mathematics, black holes, DNA molecules and parallel universes, the architect Charles Jencks has created this unusual space as living proof that logic and creativity are not always mutually exclusive.

Dubai Miracle Garden - It is hard to imagine that the biggest flower garden could appear in the middle of a desert, but for years now Dubai has been showing the world it is a land of paradoxes. Dubai Miracle Garden spreads over an area of 72,000 sq. m (775,000 sq. ft) and features more than 45 million flowers, 4 km (3 mi) of passages and walkways among the flowers, and a 1 km (1,000 yd) flower wall.

Monet's Garden at Giverny - If you've seen the painting with the lilies by the French artist Claude Monet and you wish to see it in real life, visit the artist's house just outside Paris. Water lilies blooming or not, sitting in the garden of the father of Impressionism is like becoming part of one of his paintings: the Japanese footbridge is just before you, the house and the garden have been restored to their appearance from Monet's time.

63.

Solve Mona Lisa's mysteries (*and other famous paintings*)

The Mona Lisa is one of the world's most mysterious paintings. Going through its secrets could take years of your life, so let's start with some of the main ones: Most people know that Leonardo da Vinci painted Mona Lisa, but up to this day the model herself remains a mystery. Some even say it is a female version of da Vinci himself. According to popular opinion, the lady in the painting is Lisa Gherardini, born in 1479. Why da Vinci chose her is still a mystery. Notice that Mona Lisa has no eyebrows. One of the versions is that they made a mistake during a restoration and the eyebrows disappeared. Another version is that da Vinci never finished the painting (many of his paintings remained unfinished). In 1911, the painting was stolen from the Louvre, in broad daylight, by a museum employee. It was returned two years later. Now you see why today Mona Lisa is displayed in the Louvre in a purpose-built, climate-controlled enclosure behind bulletproof glass. The painting can't be insured against theft as it is considered to be priceless and therefore uninsurable.

A couple more ideas: Solve the mysteries of other famous paintings. Girl with a Pearl Earring is in Mauritshuis, the Hague, the Netherlands. The Last Supper by Leonardo da Vinci is kept in the refectory of the Convent of Santa Maria delle Grazie, Milan (make sure you make a reservation in advance, they are usually sold out for months ahead). The famous painting with soft melting watches Persistence of Memory by Salvador Dali is kept in the Museum of Modern Art, New York City. There you will also find Starry Night by Vincent Van Gogh.

64.
Discover a beach in the middle of the city

Life is better in flip-flops, they say. If the first thing that comes to your mind when someone mentions the beach is a solitary bungalow on a remote island, we challenge you to find some of the best city beaches in the world.

A couple of ideas:

Venice Beach, Los Angeles, USA - perfect not only for sunbathing but also for renting roller skates or a bike and going down a seven-mile bike alley to Will Rogers State Beach.

Bruxelles Les Bains (Brussel Bad), Belgium - The capital of Belgium has its very own beach at Beco quay (Quai de Beco) - every year for a month a real beach appears with huge sand sets, palm-trees, exotic plants... People play beach volley and beach soccer, visitors can freely jump into fountains and all kinds of water pools.

Brygge Islands, Copenhagen, Denmark - You may think you're too far north to afford the luxury of going for a swim in the open, but that's because you haven't been to Islands Brygge - a wonderful free pool at the harbor, in central Copenhagen. The water is clear and refreshing, but you might want to jump off the quay only in July and August.

Paris Plages (Paris Beaches), France - The closest sea coast is 200 km (124 mi) from Paris but that can't stop the French. For four weeks from late July, several tons of sand are pumped onto the Seine's banks in the French capital. More than 2 km (1,5 mi) of sandy beaches invite all citizens and guests, exhausted from the heat, to a Seine-side holiday. There are free course, rollerblading, cycling, there is also a mobile library.

Repulse Bay Beach Hong Kong, China - escape from the frantic madness of Hong Kong and discover the sun and golden sands in the southern part of the island against the background of modernistic buildings and mountain slopes.

65.
Sit on colorful stairs for a happy day

Some of the world's most famous streets are in fact colorful steps, most of which keep inspiring human stories (besides, sitting on colorful steps makes for a fantastic day).

A couple of ideas:

Selaron Step (Escadaria Selaron) in Rio de Janeiro, Brazil - there are 250 steps, covered in colorful tiles from all over the world. They are the work of Chilean-born artist Jorge Selaron, who wanted to create a lively, ever changing piece of art. Today there are tiles from more than 60 countries. "This crazy and unique dream will only end on the day of my death", said Selaron once. In 2013, Selaron was found dead on the steps he had been working on for the last last 20 years of his life.

Rainbow Staircase in Istanbul, Turkey - In 2013, the retired engineer named Huseyin Cetinel decided to spruce up the neighborhoods of Findikli and Cihangir in Istanbul, redecorating many sets of steep steps in rainbow hues. Locals and tourists fell in love with the idea. No wonder smiling people flock to the artwork to take pictures.

66.
Follow the story of a song

There are places in the world which have had enough songs dedicated to them to make a long playlist for several days ahead.

A couple of ideas:

Lake Geneva and "Smoke on the Water" by Deep Purple - the band came up with the song while attending Frank Zappa's concert in Switzerland. Someone in the audience fired a Roman candle toward the ceiling and the theater caught fire, destroying the whole building as a result. The members of Deep Purple watched the show from the opposite shoreline of Lake Geneva and the "Smoke on the Water" that came to be famous song title referred to the smoke from the fire spreading over the lake. Remember this story when you visit Lake Geneva.

Iran and "Layla" by Eric Clapton - the song was written by Eric Clapton after he read "The Story of Layla and Majnun" - a Persian love story from the 12th century. Play "Layla" while visiting Iran's (once Persia) ancient monuments.

67.
Buy a book from a legendary bookstore

Not every bookstore is just a bookstore. Some are legendary and deserve your very special attention. Here are a couple of ideas. In the meantime - find your own bookstore that goes with a special story.

A couple of ideas:

Lello Bookstore, Porto, Portugal - situated in downtown Porto, this is one of the oldest in Portugal. Its two levels are connected with a huge red winding stairway. The pillars are ornamented with bronze bas-reliefs of famous figures from Portuguese literature.

Selexyz Dominicanen Bookstore in Maastricht, the Netherlands - In 2007, the first book store in a church emerged in Maastricht, the Netherlands - Selexyz Dominicanen. The Gothic church, recently turned into a temple of books, was built in 1294. In 1794, Napoleon's army took over the church as they decided it would be more godly to use it for military purposes. Since then it has been used as an archive, warehouse and parking lot for bikes before finally becoming a bookstore.

Moscow House of Books, Moscow, Russia - Novy Arbat street and the immediate vicinity is an area famous for its bookstores. Located here is the Moscow

House of Books (Dom Knigi) - the biggest bookstore in Russia with a history dating back half a century. Today they sell books here, organize holidays, festivals and charity events.

El Ateneo Grand Splendid, Buenos Aires, Argentina - It is situated in the building of the former Gran Splendid theater holding 1050 seats. Its original architecture is completely preserved - the scenery, offices, the red curtain, the balconies and the boxes. Except that there are now bookshelves where there used to be audience seats.

68.

Sweat in a valley of geysers

There are slightly more than 1000 geysers on Earth, many of which form boiling valleys. As it seems, the influence of hot water over the human mind hasn't been well studied yet because people tend to think of weird stuff to do at the geysers. Like boiling eggs (there are hundreds of videos of that; check them out, if you find it interesting).

A couple of ideas:

Yellowstone National Park, USA - thousands of hot springs, mud pots and at least 300 geysers - two-thirds of the planet's total.

The Valley of Geysers, Russia - is a lesser known

geyser field on the northern Kamchatka Peninsula, Russia with around 3000 visitors a year. But it has the second largest concentration of geysers in the world with 90 geysers and many hot springs.

The Great Geysir, Iceland - visit the geyser that gave the name to all geysers - Geysir in Iceland. The boiling water spurts out, reaching as high as 70 m (230 ft) at irregular intervals.

Fun fact... There are geysers not only on Earth. If you're planning a trip in space, you can stop by at Saturn's moon Enceladus for a water vapor eruption or go to Neptune's moon Triton for nitrogen eruptions.

69.

Drink Cachaça in Brazil and shots of coffee in Italy

Even if you don't like rum, when you go to Cuba you must have at least one shot...

How to drink as a local in...

Cuba - rum from the bottle, Cuba Libre, mojito, daiquiri (if you want to take Hemingway's advice on where to drink the last two cocktails, see Challenge 50).

Brazil - Cachaça, Caipirinha, coconut water from a

street vendor, acai (iced drink made from the acai palm tree fruit)

Greece - Ouzo, Retsina, Frappe

Turkey - Pot-boiled coffee on a stove, black tea in a tulip-shaped cup

Italy - Have an ultra-short coffee in one sip as you stand at the bar (because that's how the Italians do it), wine with dinner, digestifs after midnight.

Spain - Sangria, Calimocho (red wine and Coca Cola)

Vietnam - Ruou ran (or Snake wine - a venomous snake is placed in a glass jar of wine; it is believed to be extremely refreshing and healthy).

Norway - Practice utepils. An untranslatable world, which means to have a beer on a warm, sunny day. Those who have survived the long, cold winter days of Scandinavian countries will know how important a ritual this is for the Norwegians. Try also the strong Akvavit (alcoholic drink with spices and herbs).

70.
Eat tzatziki in Greece and gazpacho in Spain

Taking your palate on a gourmet journey is one of the most exciting adventures you can treat yourself to.

Make sure you check out the meals that are typical of the destination you're about to visit. Taste dishes that you can't have any place else. And, as they say: life is uncertain. Eat dessert first!

A couple of ideas:

Greece - Squid, roasted octopus, tzatziki, gyros, moussaka, galaktuboureko.

Italy - Fresh seafood pasta, tiramisu, lasagne, veal saltimbocca, in Naples - pizza margherita and chocolate pizza, in Sicily - Cioccolato di Modica ("Chocolate of Modica").

Spain - Tapas, tortilla de patatas in Pamplona, paella in Valencia, gazpacho in Andalusia, churros.

Thailand - Pad Thai (a fried noodle dish with meat), tom kha soup, meat and vegetables on a bamboo stick from a street vendor.

Turkey - Turkish delight, lahmajoun (Turkish pizza), iskender (kebab, served with bread, yoghurt and tomato sauce), menemen (peppers with eggs), kanafeh, pismaniye.

Where and what you would like to try:

. . . .

71.
Explore a new town with a local

The best way to explore a new place is to have a local at hand who knows all its secret little streets, delicious foods and urban legends that you won't find in guidebooks. However, you can't always find one. That's why we've prepared for you a detailed step-by-step action plan how to find yourself one of these people.

How to do it:

1. Call a friend who lives at the place you are visiting.

2. Ask around. Maybe someone you know, knows a local.

3. Book a free walk with a local guide through Global Greeters (globalgreeternetwork.info - a website that brings together locals and tourists with similar interests; you can also volunteer as a tour guide for the city you live in).

4. Post in the group of the respective town on Couchsurfing.com.

5. Post in the town groups on Facebook saying you are looking for a local to show you around and tell you stories.

6. Many towns organize free guided tours through their

information centers (check and book well in advance).

7. Join a free tour (they have these all around the world. Google the name of the town + free tour). The tour is free but you can leave a tip at the end, if you enjoyed it.

8. Hire a tour guide.

72.
Visit all seven continents

The world consists of seven continents. Of course, some are easier to reach than others (damned Antarctica!) but you have a whole life to work on it.

Mark the continents you have visited:

Europe

Asia

Africa

North America

South America

Australia

Antarctica

73.

See the Northern Lights

Unsurprisingly, viewing the Northern Lights is a dream experience for millions of travelers around the world. If it's on your list too, here's how you can see it.

When can you see the Northern Lights?

Unfortunately, you're at nature's mercy. The Northern Lights like to play hide and seek, so you'd better stick around the observation area for at least a week, at best - two weeks. Your best chance is from late August until late November and in February-March. However, the truth is, no one can guarantee when the lights will appear.

A couple of ideas: The best places to observe the Northern Lights are Norway, Canada, Greenland, Lapland, Iceland, Alaska and Sweden.

74.

Take a boat trip along Venice's canals (*or other famous canals*)

Whether on a gondola or vaporetto (Venice's public waterbus), floating along the city's canals is the best way to see it (and avoid the crowds of people in the streets).

Fun fact... It may seem like a piece of cake, but in fact navigating a gondola along Venice's canals is not that easy, and it's not for everybody. To become a gondolier, you need to undergo a long training period and the number of licenses issued a year is limited. At the exam the gondoliers-to-be need to prove their knowledge of foreign languages, the history of Venice, the sights of interest in the city and rowing. An all-male profession for centuries, in 2010 the guild accepted Giorgia Boscolo as she became the first female gondolier.

Other cities with canals that are worth visiting:

Strasbourg, France - In the beautiful neighborhood of Petite-France (Little France).

Giethoorn, the Netherlands - A town with practically no streets - only canals.

Saint Petersburg, Russia - Visit the town during the 'white nights' and see the bridges lift over the Neva river after midnight.

75.
Travel by the Trans-Siberian Railway (*or another famous train*)

Traveling by train has been a true classic for travelers ever since the time of Orient Express. And the Trans-Siberian Railway is the classic of all classics. There are two routes through Siberia. Starting the journey from Moscow, you can choose between Perm and Vladivostok. The second route takes about a week. While traveling you will enjoy the beauty of Lake Baikal and will have the chance to communicate with Russians.

Brush up a few words of Russian - written down phonetically - before you go. 'Na zdravie!' (cheers!) and 'Spasibo!' (thank you!) are great ice-breakers. (See Challenge 121)

A couple more ideas about great adventures on a train:

The Ghan, Australia - The train crosses almost 3000 km (1860 mi) through the Australian wilderness, passing through Darwin, Alice Springs and Adelaide.

El Chepe, Mexico - The train connects Chihuahua and Los Mochis. The railway crosses the desert to the north to reach as far as the Pacific Ocean. You will enjoy splendid views while traveling, such as Barranca del Cobre canyon.

Flam Railway, Norway - Very short, at high altitude, the Flam Railway connects Myrdal and Flam in Norway. While traveling you will enjoy Aurlandsfjord as well as many wild waterfalls, cascading down into the mountain hollows.

El tren de la Sierra, Peru - The train passes through the Andes and is usually called El tren de la Sierra. It connects Lima and Huancayo. This is the world's highest railway. You will see 54 bridges, 68 tunnels and make more than 1150 turns.

Rocky Mountaineer, Canada - The train flies between Vancouver and Calgary, resting at Banff and Jasper Stations. Mountains, lakes and forests take turns behind the train's window. You can spend between five and 13 nights on the train.

Bernina Express, Switzerland and Italy - From Chur in Switzerland to Tirano in Italy, Bernina Express offers four hours of magnificent mountain landscape views through the Alps. Almost 200 bridges are scattered along the route.

Orient Express, Europe - A train crossing routes, which make you daydream: Paris - Venice in one night or Paris - Istanbul in five nights, passing through Bucharest and Budapest.

76.

Drive along picturesque winding roads

Some of the most picturesque roads in the world are, unfortunately, some of the most unbearable for your "inner ear". But, oh, they're worth it!

A couple of ideas:

Big Sur, USA - or Interstate 1 is one of the best known roads in the States and you will see why, when it takes you to the breathtaking view over the Pacific Ocean. The Interstate spans 145 km (90 mi) from San Simeon to Carmel and offers wild nature and steep rocks, overlooking the waves crashing against the shore.

The Great Ocean Road, Victoria, Australia - Across a 241-kilometer (149 mi) stretch of road along the south-eastern coast of Australia, the Great Ocean Road offers a view of the ocean, blue skies and green landscapes.

Stelvio Pass, Italy - Perched at an impressive 2743 m (9000 ft), high in the Italian Alps, the road turns sharply 48 times across its relatively short span of 24 km (14 mi). Passing this road is something of a ritual for motorists and motorcyclists.

The Transfagarasan Road, Romania - Known as Ceausescu's Folly, the Transfagarasan stretches across 90 km (55 mi) of turns and curves through the highest parts of the Carpathian Mountains. It connects Sibiu and Pitesti, about 270 km (167 mi) north of Bucharest; its highest point rises to a height of 2034 m (6673 ft).

77.
Surf down an active volcano or a sand dune

Boarding is no longer restricted to snow. You can slide down far more interesting places.

Volcano Boarding is a relative newcomer among the extreme sports. It originated in Nicaragua, a country also home to the most popular destination for practising the activity - Cerro Negro volcano, the youngest active volcano in South America, only 728 m (2388 ft) high. Enthusiasts walk to the volcanic crater before proceeding to the interesting part - sliding down the volcanic stones and ash with a special board at a speed of up to 75 kph (46.6 mph). Remember to take the necessary equipment - a helmet, glasses and special overalls.

Sandboarding sends you to another, similarly warm place - the desert. Sandboarding is a sport where you slide down a sand dune with your feet fixed to a board. It is practised in Peru - Arequipa and Nazca as well as down Duna Grande (two routes - one of them 700 m (2296 ft) long, the other - 1 km (3280 ft). In Australia try the Dunes of Lucky Bay with its trained beginners instructors. In Chile go to Valle de la Muerte, they also practice sandboarding in Dubai Desert and Namib Desert in Namibia. Currently in Europe there's one place for sandboarding - Hirschau artificial sand hills in Germany.

78.

Hug a kangaroo (*or koala, or another animal*)

There are plenty of zoos and animal centers where the inhabitants are not behind the bars of a cage, and you can get really close to them. If hugging a kangaroo or another wild animal is your dream, remember you need to be extra careful not to stress them out.

79.

Have a drink at an ice bar

Put on your snowboots and fluffy headphones and order a drink at a bar where you won't need ice with your drink...

A couple of ideas: Some of the world's best ice bars are in Jukkasjärvi, Sweden, at Hotel de Glace (Quebec,

Canada), Chillout Bar (Dubai), Bar Minus 5 (New York, USA), Aurora Ice Bar (Alaska, USA), Xtracold Ice Bar (Amsterdam, the Netherlands), Ice Club Roma (Rome, Italy).

80.
Stand before the gates of Hell

If you are a true adventurer, you would hardly be worried by the challenge of going to the Gate of Hell in Turkmenistan. They don't allow people in, but who would like to go inside anyway...

What is the Gate of Hell?

It's a crater, 60 m (196 ft) in diameter and 20 m (65 ft) deep, burning across its entire surface. Its real name is Darvaza and it's man-made, however not by some religious fanatics in search of the inferno. It resulted from a Russian gas extraction project not long ago in 1971. During drilling, the rig fell into a subterranean cave and released underground natural gas reserves. To avoid a further environmental catastrophe, the former Soviet Union authorities thought it best to cover the place with natural glass. The plan was: "It will burn and burn, burning off eventually in three to four days"... and so the crater continues to burn day and night to this today.

The Gate of Hell is located in the middle of the Karakum

Desert, about three hours along a dirt road from the capital Ashgabat. Go there at night for the most impressive experience.

81.
Go up in a balloon

Ever since the Montgolfier brothers succeeded in launching their balloon (named deservedly after them - the montgolfier) into the air in 1782, we've been drawn up into the sky. See the world as the birds see it. Take to the skies at dawn above Angkor Wat in Cambodia, over the rock wonders of Cappadocia or in the Dubai Desert - pick your destination and rise at dawn as the view is the most beautiful then.

Where you dream of flying in a balloon:
. . . .

82.
Breathe in the scent of lavender in Provence

From June until August, Provence in France holds a feast of the senses with its dark purple lavender fields. Some lavender producers offer tours among the flower beds as well as natural products made from the herbs, wine tastings, jam and what not.

83.
Visit a concentration camp... *never to go back there again*

Traveling isn't only about having a coffee, visiting museums and relaxing under the shade of a palm tree. It's also about those historic locations, which may seem terrifying, yet they imperceptibly transform your understanding of the world. Yes, these are the death camps and yes, they aren't a top tourist destination. Many people even avoid them to escape the heavy burden. However, parts of these camps are now museums with the sole purpose of showing the horror so that the world never goes back there again.

A couple of ideas: Auschwitz concentration camp - known also as Oswiecim, is the biggest death camp, several kilometers from the Polish town of Krakow. Dachau concentration camp is 10 km (6 mi) from Munich, Germany. Sachsenhausen concentration camp is 30 minutes from Berlin, Germany. Buchenwald concentration camp is 10 km (6 mi) from Weimar, Germany.

84.

Welcome the young wine

Beaujolais Nouveau and the third Thursday of November have been intertwined for years - earlier only in France, recently in many other places as well. Many towns organize events in honor of the young wine's arrival. And the young beaujolais doesn't arrive unannounced, but rather as a noble figure - marked by parties and impatient greeters.

The tradition of celebrating the new harvest (of the Gamay grape variety) was established by wine producers from the French town of Beaujeu in the beginning of 19th century. Since 1985, the celebrations have taken place on the third Thursday of November every year, regardless of when the wine was harvested. On the stroke of midnight it is announced: "Le Beaujolais Nouveau est arrivé!" (The new beaujolais has arrived!"), and tastings of the young wine follow - in bars, cafes, restaurants...

You must taste the beaujolais while it's still young - between November and March. Because of the accelerated fermentation, its taste is unique every year. By law, all grapes must be harvested by hand.

85.

Walk the narrowest streets in the world

Skip breakfast on the day you decide to squeeze through some of the narrowest streets in the world, because most of them look like a crevice rather than something that is supposed to have an official name on the city's map.

A couple of ideas:

Spreuerhofstraße in the Old Town of Reutlingen, Germany. At its narrowest point it is only 31 cm (12.2 in) wide. This is, in fact, the world's narrowest street according to the Guinness World Records. Spreuerhofstraße was built in 1727.

Strada Sforii in Brasov, Romania is 109 cm (42.9 in) at its narrowest point. Translated into English, the name means "String Street". It was built in the 15th century as a corridor that firemen could use.

The narrowest street in Italy doesn't even have a name. When you arrive in the medieval town of Ripatransone, ask the locals or follow the signs to the alley, which is only 35 cm (13.7 in) at its narrowest part. You can get a certificate from the tourist office as proof that you walked along the street.

Parliament Street in Exeter, England is 64 cm (25 in) wide in its narrowest part. Some time ago the residents in the area asked the local authorities to widen it, but, apparently, it never happened.

86.

Discover your philosophy of a happy life while traveling

You don't have to be a philosopher to find a brand new philosophy of a happy life, and experience it as you travel free from cares and non-philosophically. In many places in the world, they've had it figured for many years.

A couple of ideas:

Pura vida in Costa Rica - Pura vida simply translated in English is "pure life", but the phrase actually has a far deeper meaning. Costa Ricans use it to say hello, to say bye or as an answer to the question "How are you?". Pura vida is in fact a way of life, where you accept that no matter how difficult, your life is not that bad at all.

Dolce far niente in Italy - Literally means "sweet doing nothing" and the Italians, especially in the southern part of the country, know how to turn idleness into a happy occupation. This philosophy of life contains a number of important prohibitions, such as no haste, no taking problems to heart and no paying attention to the surrounding nuisance.

Hakuna matata in Africa - Thanks to the animated film "The Lion King" everybody knows a bit of Swahili. Hakuna matata means "no problem", "no worries". The phrase is used mainly in Kenya and Zanzibar.

Tri Hita Karana in Bali - If harmony means happiness, then this philosophy of life from Bali will help you achieve it. In English Tri Hita Karana means "three reasons for well-being" - being in harmony with people, in harmony with God and in harmony with nature.

Friluftsliv in Norway - There's no such thing as bad weather, only inappropriate clothing. True to this principle, the Norwegians are fans of friluftsliv or life in "free" air ("open-air living"). The northern country's inhabitants appreciate the benefits of spending time in the open for health and well-being, regardless of weather conditions. Whether it is running, cycling or just going out to the park nearby to take some photos - the important thing is to breathe fresh air.

Wabi-Sabi in Japan - Salvador Dali once said "Have no fear of perfection - you'll never reach it". This is exactly what the Japanese idea Wabi-Sabi tries to convey. In English it means "accept imperfection" and applies to the individual body and character, friends and life in general.

Fernweh in Germany - English doesn't have an antonym of "nostalgia" but in German it's "Fernweh". It means a strong desire for traveling, dreaming of far and unknown lands and new experiences. So give in to your Fernweh and hit the road.

87.

Bargain at an exotic market

Bargaining is the best part of going to exotic markets. You and the vendor outwitting each other, laughing, talking about all sorts of unrelated things, they treat you with tea or coffee... In the end, you leave with a story to tell, pleased that you struck the bargain of your life (though it often doesn't turn out like that).

Bargain tips:

1. Find out how much locals pay and refuse to pay more than that (ask a trusted local or take a peek over the shoulder of the buyer in front of you). For instance, state craft shops and hotel gift shops generally have fixed (high) prices, which will give you an idea of the upper real price limit range of goods.

2. If the vendor's initial offer is significantly higher, you can laugh. This will quickly show that you're aware of the true price.

3. Just as vendors often start with ridiculously high prices, you can offer a way lower price than you expect

to finally pay. This allows you to negotiate.

4. If you've made up your mind to buy something, you might as well say goodbye to the vendor, showing that you won't continue with the negotiations and you're leaving. This will guarantee you at least two more new prices, each lower than the one before. In a different turn of events, they might ask you "Ok, how much would you give?", which means that the vendor is sensing that the potential sale is slipping away.

5. If there's two of you or more, you can act it out. You want the goods but your friend keeps the money and won't let you pay so much, or something of the sort.

6. Be polite and friendly (but firm) in the negotiations. If the vendor likes you, you will most probably strike a good bargain.

7. They may offer you tea, coffee, something to eat, etc. You can accept but this doesn't mean you have to buy it. Still, they may try to make you feel guilty. Stay firm.

8. Learn to count in the local language and you can win some respect, whence a better price. Stick to the local language, if you can, even if the vendor speaks to you in English or your own language.

9. Remember that usually vendors aren't evil frauds trying to take people's hard-earned money. Often these are just businesspeople working to support their family. By bargaining you're not aiming to cut their profit but to reach a price that satisfies both sides.

10. Don't take it too seriously.

88.

Walk hundreds of miles along a pilgrimage route

Today these routes are more for tourists than pilgrims. No matter what inspires you to walk hundreds of miles, to cycle or ride a horse, it's a significant achievement.

A couple of ideas around the world:

The spring of the river Ganges, India - They say more than 10 million people walk the way to the sacred water every year. Those who are determined to reach the very spring, need to go to the western part of the Himalayas. For Indian Hindus, the Ganges embodies divinity and purity. Legend has it that the waters of the river purify all sins of the people who touch it.

Camino de Santiago, France/Spain - The Camino de Santiago, also known as El Camino, is a religious route attracting more and more enthusiasts. The unforgettable journey may continue more than one month, starting from France through the Pyrenees and crossing the whole of Spain. The last point is the cathedral in Santiago de Compostela, as it is believed that St. James's remains were buried there. The length of the route may vary, depending on where you start. The route from France to the famous cathedral is almost 800 km (497 mi).

Visit Medina, Saudi Arabia - Medina is a holy Muslim city, the second most important city after Mecca. Medina attracts millions of pilgrims every year, because it contains the remains of the Islamic prophet Muhammad. In Medina, you can see the three oldest mosques in the world, one of which is the Prophet's Mosque.

Walk the Inca Trail to Machu Picchu, Peru - The Inca Trail consists of three trails - Mollepata (six or seven days), Classic (four or five days), and One Day. Regardless of which trail you choose, you will see many ruins of the Inca civilization before reaching Machu Picchu Mountain itself. Concerns about overuse, harming the nature and the historical sites along the way, led the Peruvian government to limit the number of tourists allowed to hike this trail to 200. As a result, advance booking is mandatory. More information on www.machupicchu.gob.pe.

89.

Ride a camel in the desert or a donkey in Greece

The truth is, most people who didn't grow up among herds of camels, say they would never ride a desert animal again. This, however, shouldn't stop you from trying something different.

Watch out: Camels have the unpleasant habit of spitting at tourists. How can you find out you are about to have a close encounter with the spit of a camel? If you notice that the camel lifts its head and after that sticks its tongue out - take to your heels, because the next phase is shooting out spit, at great speed and distance.

A couple of ideas: In all Arab countries you can ride a camel and travel through dunes like a Bedouin. In Southeast Europe (Greece, Romania, Bulgaria and others) explore the mountains on the back of a donkey. In fact, if you haven't ridden a horse, you can start from there. Go dog sledding in winter in the Nordic countries.

90.

Get close to the bowels of the earth in a salt mine

How do you feel about a several-hour walk deep under the ground in the galleries of a salt mine? In many places around the world, old salt mines are now open to tourists. You don't have to lick the walls to see if they're salty - we already did it.

Why do it: Your little excursion to the salt mines is not only exciting but also healthy. Take a deep breath because you can breathe more easily there due to salt vapors - many salt mines have built-in treatment centers.

A couple of ideas:

The Wieliczka Salt Mine in Poland is located 10 km (6 mi) from Krakow. It is 327 m (1072 ft) deep, tourists are allowed 135 m (442 ft) underground (to level three out of a total of nine levels). You will see salt formations, exquisite salt statues, underground lakes, several underground churches and will also learn about legends and stories. At 123 m (403 ft) underground, there is a restaurant.

Turda Salt Mine in Romania is located in the northern part of the country, in the city of Turda. There is a real underground amusement park across several levels among the natural set of the mine, which creates the feeling that you're traveling to the Center of the Earth. In the middle of a huge cavity underground (15 floors deep), an enormous Ferris wheel rises. It turns very gently and slowly so that you can see the mine from every angle. Salina Turda also boasts a mini-golf, bowling alley, row boats and the favorite of all visitors - panoramic elevators.

The Salt Cathedral in Colombia - Near present-day Zipaquirá, a town in the Andes, they have been extracting salt since ancient times. In 1954, however, a real architectural miracle was built inside the salt mine - a cathedral dedicated to the Patron saint of miners Our Lady of Rosary. Today there is a second cathedral below the first and it holds up to 8000 people. It is located near Parque de la Sal (Salt Park) with its museum of mining.

91.

Attend a tea ceremony in Japan, England or Morocco

Drinking tea in many places around the world can be a truly special experience.

A couple of ideas:

Tea ceremony in Japan - it hasn't changed much since the time of emperors. Dedicate at least two hours (sometimes up to four) and prepare to perform the series of rituals. They organize tea ceremonies in all big cities in the country.

Mint tea in Morocco, Algeria or Tunisia - Here they have green tea with fresh mint leaves, very strongly sweetened. The ceremony includes pouring the tea several times from the pot into the cup and back. Have in mind that the tea, of which they usually serve at least three cups, is a symbol of hospitality and it's rude to refuse.

Tea with milk at 3 pm in England - The British drink 165 million cups of tea every day. In the morning, at lunch, during a break... However, the most authentic, the most British is the three o'clock tea. Traditionally, it is served in the good company of cakes, jam-filled scones and tuna and cucumber sandwiches. Milk is a must (only 2% of English people drink their tea without milk, surveys show).

Why the English drink tea at 3 pm - Why the English drink tea at 3 pm - According to British urban legends, drinking tea at 3 pm was "invented" by Anna Maria, wife of the seventh Duke of Bedford. The reason couldn't be more trivial - the Duchess would get so hungry between lunch at 1 pm and dinner at 7 pm that she would drink tea and have a light snack in the afternoon. To make it more interesting she decided to invite friends over to keep her company and gradually it turned into a tradition. In less than 20 years afternoon tea as a social event spread across the whole of England, with all the ostentation and noble over-refinement that the female representatives of the English elite society could put into it. Tea was served in the finest porcelain together with tiny plates of sandwiches, cakes and scones.

92.

Discover a desert where you least expect it

Sometimes deserts play tricks on us and appear where we least expect them. Mix up your senses with one of the desert landscapes below that can be found at unexpected places or are simply deserts out of place.

A couple of ideas:

The Great Dune of Pyla in France is the tallest sand dune in Europe. It is about 500 m (1640 ft) wide, 3 km

(1 mi) long, with an average height of 107 m (351 ft), constantly moving. The dune moves towards land and slowly pushes the forest back to cover houses and the nearby road. Sometimes it moves 10 m (33 ft) a year, sometimes only 1 m (3 ft). If you are lucky enough, you can see it covered in snow. It is located 60 km (37.5 mi) from Bordeaux, France.

Loonse en Drunense Duinen is a national park in the Netherlands, just a few kilometers from Tilburg, which very much reminds us of a desert with its sand and dunes. Interestingly enough, the road to the dunes passes through a small coniferous forest.

The Simpson Desert, Australia is unique with its rusty orange sands, incredibly beautiful at sunset.

HAPPINESS CHALLENGES TO HELP YOU FIND YOURSELF

"People travel to wonder at the height of the mountains, at the huge waves of the seas, at the long course of the rivers, at the vast compass of the ocean, at the circular motion of the stars, and yet they pass by themselves without wondering."
—Saint Augustine

"What can we gain by sailing to the moon if we are not able to cross the abyss that separates us from ourselves? This is the most important of all voyages of discovery, and without it, all the rest are not only useless, but disastrous."
—Thomas Merton

93.
The random stop challenge

Set out at least once on a journey with only one point on your itinerary - the starting point. Sometimes it's good to leave things to fate. And fate always has interesting ideas about who and what to introduce you to.

How to do it:

By train - Go to the station and catch the next train. Get off at the third (or fourth, or tenth...) stop. You can take your bike with you and return on two wheels.

By car - Take a friend, ask them to close their eyes and give you random directions such as "pass three exits and turn left".

By car II - Go in a random direction with a clear idea where to turn (for example, at the first sign with a weird name of a village, at the third possible exit, etc.).

What to do when you arrive:
Get off with no expectations. Release your senses. Talk to people. Have a beer/tea with them. Ask them about interesting places and local stories. If you end up at an event (fair, celebration), join in.

94.

It's a big world and free stuff lurks just around the corner

Those who say traveling is expensive are just ill-informed. We challenge you to take advantage of as many free things as possible while you travel.

A couple of ideas:

Free fun on your birthday - Traveling on your birthday is worth it. Wherever you go - many sights of interest around the world offer special birthday discounts.
For example: you can ride the Table Mountain Aerial Cableway to Table Mountain above Cape Town for free. Or, wherever you are, just ask what birthday discounts they offer.

Free museum admission - Almost every museum in the world has a free admission day (for example, every second Thursday of the month). Check it out and take the opportunity, if possible.

Free museums in Paris - All public museums in Paris are free for EU citizens under the age of 26.

The best free attractions in the world - Some of the most popular attractions in the world are free. **The Staten Island Ferry** in New York is the perfect way to enjoy the panorama of Ellis Island, the Statue of Liberty, the Hudson River and Manhattan. **The British Museum in London** not only keeps some of the world's greatest treasures but is also free and allows photography inside. **The Berlin Wall Memorial** in Berlin, the **Berardo Museum in Lisbon** (with works by Dali, Picasso and Andy Warhol), the **National Museum of Denmark** in Copenhagen and the **Victoria and Albert Museum** in London are also on the list.

Learn foreign languages for free to communicate more while abroad - There are plenty of websites that offer free online foreign language lessons to help you communicate more with locals when you travel.

Although you have to pay for additional functions and higher levels, the basic levels are free of charge. Try DuoLingo, Omniglot, My Language Exchange or Lang-8.

Free museums and galleries in Italy - From 2015 every first Sunday of the month, all public museums and galleries in Italy are free, including the Colosseum, Uffizi Gallery and Pompeii Ruins. But be prepared to wait.

Free food - The are several places in Paris that will gladly serve your drink with free food (couscous, fried clams) - bar La Cordonnerie, bar Le Grenier, the oriental bar Le Tribal Cafe. Google "A free meal at a bar in Paris" to find the addresses as well as other similar bars and restaurants. Bars in Milan and many cities in northern Italy offer the so-called "aperitivo hour" (look for the sign). Usually after 7 pm, when you order a cocktail in a bar, you may get a free access to a buffet table with bites.

Free accommodation - There are several ways to find free accommodation. One option is to use sites like Couchsurfing and Hospitality Club, where millions of hospitable users from all over the world will offer you their homes while you visit their city or village. In exchange, you give them your friendship, nice conversations and a cooked meal from your country (many a moussaka has been cooked around the world by the authors of this book!). You need to create an account. You can register on one of the many home exchange, house sitting and pet sitting websites that give you the chance to exchange your home for somebody else's. Another option: If you're traveling from one city to another, take the night train/bus to save money and time to walk around the city. Free accommodation in Italy: In autumn in Italy during Barter Week you can barter goods and services for your stay in a vast number of the Italian bed & breakfasts (en.settimanadelbaratto.it). Almost everywhere you can get free accommodation for volunteer work.

95.
The fear challenge

Do something that scares you. For example, learn to ride a bike/ to snowboard/ to water ski. Overcome the embarrassment and speak in a foreign language with a foreigner. Try rock climbing with an instructor. It's important to try, rather than to succeed. This is the first step towards dealing with your fears.

Two types of fear: There are two types of fear. The first is the fear that makes your heart beat faster when you see a car going at 120 kph (74.5 mph) coming right at you. This fear saves your ass by making you move away. The other type is the fear that stops you from doing something you want because "But what if bla, bla, bla?". What if... But what if... Trying to do its job to keep you out of harm's way, sometimes your brain screws you.

How to do it: This is nature's work - the fear of something you haven't done before. If you're afraid, remember that thousands of people around the world have done it before you, and they are absolutely ordinary people. You're afraid, not because it's really scary (just to remind you that you have no idea what it's going to be like!), but because you're facing something unfamiliar. Fear also means that you're about to experience something great and once you do it, you will tell yourself: "Wow! Was it really me who did that?! Was I really afraid?!".

So do a list of the things you're afraid to do, set a deadline and make a plan for small steps towards overcoming your fear. You can take veeery small steps. It's important to keep moving.

The fear you want to overcome:

. . . .

96.

Keep a diary of your travels or start a blog

Instead of passport stamps, start counting those moments on the road that you don't want to forget. On paper, in a scrapbook, in a file or blog - travel memories deserve a place to be collected and preserved. Why not together with a treasure box with memories from visited destinations.

1. You relive the beautiful moments as you put them in writing.

2. You can't rely on your memory - there are moments and details that fade with time.

3. Also, write down phone numbers, hotel names, nice restaurants and other useful information, which may help a friend who follows in your footsteps a few years later.

97.

Remember what you loved to do when you were a child

When we are young, we create traditions and think of ways to have fun on school trips or family vacations. What was your favorite activity as a child (collecting seashells on the beach, drawing the most exciting thing of the day, running across meadows, climbing trees...)? Do it at your next trip.

98.

Say "yes" if a stranger invites you for coffee

If you often travel to faraway villages and towns, you must have been invited, on several occasions, to have coffee with a stranger after exchanging only a few sentences. The automatic reaction of today's typical urban dweller would be to turn down that offer (1. doesn't want to disturb the stranger 2. doesn't want to change the plan). The automatic reaction of the true traveler would be to accept the offer.

Why do it: If you were disturbing this stranger, they wouldn't have invited you to have coffee together. In small villages and towns, where everybody knows one another, new people (yes, that's you!) are interesting and bring something different. If you're not in a great hurry, stay for a coffee. Once, in a remote village, a similar situation, only 15 minutes later, turned into our host's attempt to set up his grandson with one of the girls in our group. To this day, it's been a great story to tell friends.

99.
The low-value notes challenge

Pick a low-value banknote or a coin (one-dollar note/one-euro coin). For a whole year, put every such note that comes into your possession in a big money box or jar. You can't spend it (even if they ask you in the store because they can't give you enough change). When the year has passed, count the money and you will be surprised how much you've saved without even noticing. Use the money to travel.

The amount you saved in a year:

. . . .

100.

Be spontaneous! Follow an interesting sign and change the plan

The ability to give up plans to venture into the unknown is directly proportional to the ability to enjoy traveling (and life) in general.

101.

Put your dream destinations on a board to help make them come true

Make a vision board with your dream destinations. Take a cork or whatever other board, stick up photos, graphics, postcards, even whole phrases or articles connected with the place you dream about. Put it in a place, where you will see it every day.

Why do it: Simply put, we humans are incredibly busy creatures and get constantly distracted, even from our dreams. It is proven that we are much more likely to realize our dreams if we keep them in sight. Why?

Because we focus and our brain gets tuned accordingly, which means it catches every useful opportunity it would otherwise have missed.

Watch out: Your goals need to be as specific as possible. "I want to travel" is too general. Which are the places you have the strongest desire to visit? What exactly is it that you want to do there?

Other ideas: Hang a map of the world and pin every destination you visit. The best decorations in a traveler's home are their memories and dreams. Bring the two into one place by marking the destinations you have already visited as well as those you dream of visiting. Use pins in different colors.

102.
Learn something new while you travel

Always when you travel, try to learn at least one new thing.

A couple of ideas: There are thematic cooking classes in many places (France, Italy), lessons, workshops and all kinds of courses. Photography classes are a great idea as you will be visiting wonderful places and will be able to take more and more beautiful pictures. Check what's happening in and around the place you're going to, ask in museums and galleries - you usually need to sign up several days earlier.

103.
Inspire your children to travel

If you want your children to be greater travelers even than yourself, you need to take care of it while they are at a very early age by constantly nurturing their curiosity, independence and adventurous spirit. Don't be surprised when they start traveling the planet and on Christmas day give you a phone call from the other end of the world.

A couple of ideas:

1. Give them a huge map of the world, an illustrated atlas or a globe.

2. Ask them to make a list of their dream destinations for a vacation.

3. Ask them to make a list (with words or drawings) of the things they would like to see and do during their vacation.

4. Include them in the preparations for the trip (make them pack their bags, put napkins with the sandwiches, etc.).

5. Give them their own little travel backpack, where they can put their favorite toy, game, pencils and drawing paper.

104.

Turn traveling into a profession

Never again will you say that you don't have enough time to travel. There are plenty of professions that entail lots of traveling - of the kind that allow you truly to have fun. Many others leave you with enough free time or offer flexible working hours so that you can work whenever and wherever you wish.

A couple of ideas: Freelance journalist (photographer, designer, programmer, translator), flight attendant, pilot, yacht sailor, cruise ship staff, geologist, tour guide, tourist agent, import/export trader.

105.

Walk on hot coals
(*or watch how others do it*)

The tradition of walking and dancing on hot coals has

existed in distant corners of the world for centuries. These rituals used to be mystical, magical while today... well, we wouldn't like to spoil all the magic, but google "How to walk over hot coals" and you will see there is science behind the ritual.

A couple of ideas:
Watch traditional rituals of walking on smouldering embers in Bulgaria (nestinari, or the people who walk and dance on embers, on the evening of the 3rd of June in the village of Bulgari), Greece (Anastenaria, from the 21st to 23rd of May in five villages in northern Greece), India (by Indians in Tamil Nadu, who celebrate Thimithi in October or November). It is also practiced by the Kung people in the Kalahari Desert, tribes in Polynesia and San Pedro Manrique residents in Spain (23rd June).

106.
Visit the country this book comes from

The authors of this book invite you to visit the country where the book was inspired and created - Bulgaria. It is situated on the Balkan Peninsula, in the eastern part of Europe.

10 of our favorite experiences in Bulgaria:

Travel at 30 kph (20 mph) on the legendary narrow gauge railway (tesnolineyka) through three mountain ranges.

Do a pagan dance with kukeri (or mummers - men, wearing costumes and masks, perform traditional rituals to scare evil spirits away) - in early January or during Sirni Zagovezni (a winter holiday to celebrate forgiveness, seven weeks before the Orthodox Easter, always on Sunday).

Climb the highest peak in the country - Musala (2925 m/ 9596.45 ft), which means "close to God".

Join the traditional horo (a type of circle folk dance) in the icy waters of the Tundzha river in the town of Kalofer on 6th January - traditionally only men can participate.

Pick roses before sunrise in June in the Rose Valley, near the town of Kazanlak.

Taste wines of Bulgarian grape varieties among the vineyards (our favorite local wine varieties include Gamza, Mavrud, Pamid, Shiroka Melnishka (broad-leaved Melnik), Rubin, Misket).

Listen to Bulgarian bagpipes at the biggest bagpipe festival in the Rhodope Mountain - in the village of Gela, on the first Saturday of August.

Learn about the life of the ancient Thracians in some of their most beautiful tombs (the tombs in Sveshtari (UNESCO), Starosel, Mezek, the Tomb of Seuthes III near Kazanlak).

Explore the mystery of how the Stone Desert (Pobiti Kamani) was formed.

Try traditional Bulgarian cuisine - tarator, kyufte, kebapche, banitsa, patatnik, shopska salad, lyutenitsa, mekitsa (google each one of these for more information or trust us blindly and order one straight away!). Something to drink - a shot of strong rakia is a good start.

107.
Recreate your childhood memories

Pick your favorite photos from your childhood. Go to the places where they were taken and pose for a photo to replicate the original. See how the world has (not) changed while you were growing up.

108.

Spend Christmas at 30°C (*85°F*) or celebrate a traditional holiday in a non-traditional way

Traditions are to be changed from time to time. Bring something different into your life (and that of your loved ones) by turning a classical holiday upside down. It will certainly be a holiday everyone will be talking about for years to come.

A couple of ideas:

Christmas at 30°C (85°F) - If you live in the Northern Hemisphere and, for you, Christmas equals snow, choose an exotic destination with warm weather at least once, but don't forget your Santa hat for a photo shoot on the beach. If you live in the Southern Hemisphere, change palm trees and heat with snow and pine trees.

Christmas in the wild - Gather the family in the camper van and go to a forest, lake or another favorite place. Decorate with Christmas lights, light a fire and enjoy the different experience.

New Year's, camping in the desert - Mark the beginning of the new year with Bedouin cuisine, music and dances around the campfire in the middle of the desert. Spend the night in a tent camp among sand dunes and get up at dawn to welcome the first sunrise of a great new year in your life. There are similar tours in Jordan, Dubai, Morocco, India - prices, duration and extras included may vary.

109.

Forget your camera

You are looking through the photos from a trip and you see for the first time something you hadn't noticed when you were there. Sounds familiar? When you see something beautiful, your first reaction is to take a picture of it. If you spend the whole time taking pictures, however, it turns out in the end that you saw the place through the lens, not with your eyes.

How to do it: This time forget that you have a camera and just enjoy. Set aside several hours only for contemplating, listening, breathing... Create memories no one else knows about. They will be yours alone. If you insist on photos, ask someone in your group to take them instead.

110.

Use your talents to preserve memories from your trips

It's not important what talents you have. What counts is the desire to give a part of yourself. Draw what you see. Write a poem/story/travelogue. Write down a stream of words and thoughts that come into your head at that very moment. Gather pine cones, stones, flowers and create decorations with your hands.

111.

Just when you're thinking of turning something down, say "yes" at the last minute

If you randomly opened at this page and randomly landed on this number, we challenge you to accept the next suggestion you would normally say "no" to.

For seasoned travelers: Accept any suggestion for a whole day/week.

112.

Get lost on purpose

Getting lost in an unknown city is the best way to find interesting things and experiences, to meet interesting people (who are rarely among the crowds of tourists) and come across unexpected treasures.

Try to get lost in a familiar city. To do this you will have to find small streets where you haven't been before, and feel the thrill of not knowing where you are.

113.

The slow return challenge

Choose a destination and go there as quickly as possible. But on the way back home choose the slowest possible transport and way of returning. Change the several-hour flight for a several-day exciting trip. Stop, change transport, take detours, postpone your arrival - even if only by five minutes. Enjoy every place, every encounter and situation on the road.

114.

Try NOT to travel for 3/6/12 months

This is a challenge for the most addicted travelers, which is much more difficult than ordinary people might think. Use the time to save for a major trip after that.

Why do it: Did you know that there is a disease called

dromomania, which generally means inability of the patient to stop moving from one place to the other. The impulse is so strong that the 'sick' person can't resist and travels all the time. So, do you suffer from dromomania?

115.

You want a raise?
Take a holiday!

It is a proven fact that employees who use more of their vacation days achieve better results at work and have a higher chance of being promoted. Many people don't use all of their vacation days as they fear that their long absence might show their bosses that the work can be managed without them.

A study, however, shows that employees, who take all of their vacation days, show better results at work. Statistics in the USA and Canada reveal that for every 10 days off from work, the employee's results improve by an average of 8%.

How to do it (if your boss won't give you a holiday): Show this page to your boss (or an employee who urgently needs to take a break)...

116.

Travel more often for shorter periods of time instead of rarely for longer periods

Traveling often in small bites proves to be good for your mood, happiness and satisfaction in life.

Why do it: A number of studies show that if we do the things we love often and in small doses, we feel happier than if we wait for a long time for the things that give us pleasure, so that we can devote more time to them. This is because the brain has the property of "getting used to" nice things and after a certain period no longer values them as exciting and unusual. Despite some discrepancies between the different studies, it is considered that the perfect holiday, from which body and mind benefit the most, is between three and eight days.

117.

Go on a two-week trip only with a backpack, weighing not more than 10 kg (*22 lbs*)

In this challenge for seasoned travelers you have to pack the absolute minimum amount of luggage that you might need on a two-week trip to a warm country.

What you need: Some light clothes (you can wash them while you travel), basic hygiene accessories, basic medicines, a big scarf, a thin towel, camera, phone, chargers, passport and money. You can do without the rest.

For seasoned travelers: A one-month trip with a backpack not more than 7 kg (15 lbs), which is the restriction on cabin luggage of some airline companies.

118.

Become a volunteer

Choose a cause and become a volunteer. Usually that means a free ride, food and accommodation, as well as free entry (if you volunteer at a festival). Whether you plant trees, clean a national park or build a festival stage, new encounters and the pleasant feeling of being part of a cause are guaranteed.

Why do it: Many studies show that there is a direct causal relationship between doing a selfless good deed and feeling happy. Yes! It seems that the best way to make yourself happy is… to make others happy.

A couple of ideas: Besides volunteering for cleaning campaigns or festivals, you can volunteer for long-term projects abroad. Volunteering as a way of traveling gives you the opportunity to spend between several weeks and several months in a foreign country, to contribute to the development of local communities, and, at the same time, to gain valuable experience and skills and find new friends.

119.

Travel instead of taking pills

Among all other things, traveling is healthy too. So the next time someone asks you how come you never stop, you have every right to say: for health reasons. Here are a few highlights of scientific studies over the past years:

Traveling works almost instantly like a pill. Only two

days of holiday are enough to drastically decrease the body's levels of stress.

Women who go on holiday less often than twice a year face a higher risk of suffering a heart attack.

Men who do not use all of their vacation days are 30% more susceptible to cardiovascular diseases.

120.

Close your eyes, turn the map of your country three times and then point to a place

Open your eyes and discover your destination for next weekend.

Why do it: Because usually the most interesting destinations are the most unexpected ones. Besides, you don't seem to have any other ideas right now!

121.

Learn and use a few basic phrases in the local language

There is nothing like speaking to a foreigner for 10 minutes in English, after which he twists his tongue to tell you in your native language "thank you" (if English is not your mother tongue). Uttering words in the local language is a sure device for breaking the ice, getting discounts at markets and dinner invitations when you're abroad. So, make the effort to learn the local way of saying "Hello", "Thank you", "Excuse me", "Very tasty" (this phrase in particular has assured us not one and two free desserts!). Even if you know only five words in the language of the country you're visiting, beer religion requires one of them to be "Cheers!". Because, as we know, alcohol brings people together, overcomes language barriers and creates friendships in seconds.

If the language you need is not on the list, use body language - raise your glass with a broad smile.

How to say "Cheers" in 45 languages

Albania	Gëzuar
Armenia	Genatzt
Azerbaijan	Nuş olsun
Bosnia and Herzegovina	Živjeli
Bulgaria	Наздраве [Nazdrave]
Burma	Aung myin par say
China (Mandarin)	干杯, gān bēi
Croatia	Živjeli/Nazdravlje
Czech Republic	Na zdravi
Denmark	Skål
Egypt	Fee sihetak
Estonia	Terviseks
Finland	Kippis
France	Santé
Germany	Prost/Zum vohl
Greece	Γεια μας /Gia mas
Hawaii	Å' kålè ma' luna
Hungary	Egészségedre
Iceland	Skál
Ireland (Gaelic)	Sláinte
Israel	Ľchaim
Italy	Salute/Cin cin
Japan	Kanpai

Korea	Gun bae
Latvia	Priekā/Prosit
Lithuania	į sveikatą
Morocco	Saha wa'afiab
Mongolia	Tulgatsgaaya
Norway	Skål
Poland	Na zdrowie
Portugal	Saúde
Romania	Noroc
Russia	Наздоровье [Nazdarovye]
Serbia	Živeli
Slovakia	Na zdravie
Slovenia	Na zdravje
Spain	Salud
Sweden	Skål
Thailand	Chon
The Netherlands	Proost
The Philippines	Mabuhay
South Africa (Afrikaans)	Gesondheid
Turkey	Şerefe
Ukraine	Будьмо [Budmo]
Vietnam	Dô/Vô

122.

Ask a local about their favorite place to eat

The best strategy to find a good place to eat isn't actually the Internet and all its applications for sharing visitors' opinions (the fake comments are more numerous than you might think). Go offline and ask someone in the street which their favorite place to eat is (to drink, to listen to live music or play billiards). You can ask several people so that you have a backup plan (the receptionist at the hotel/hostel, the vendor, etc.).

123.

Spend 45 minutes in a soundproof room

Imagine a room that isolates 99.9% of sound. Imagine you're in that room, alone in the dark. You can hear your heartbeat and, after a few minutes in the room, even your lungs! In the soundproof room you become the sound. According the Guinness World Records this is the quietest place on Earth.

How to do it: This is a really serious challenge. They have such rooms in some universities in Great Britain and USA, and they keep opening new and new rooms in different places in the world. Usually, they announce several visiting days throughout the year. Google "anechoic chamber" + country or town, closest to you.

124.

The art of traveling solo and why to do it

Until recently, it was considered that only losers, who obviously have zero friends in the whole wide world, are forced by their wretched fate to drag themselves alone along the paths of the planet. Today, traveling solo is perceived as a more normal phenomenon, one that we recommend you practice at least once a year.

Why do it:

1. When you're alone, you have no one else to consider but yourself, and you can do only what you really want. Like spend hours in a gallery or aimlessly roam the small streets of a city or village.

2. You have time to put your thoughts in order and have important conversations with yourself.

3. When you're alone, you're much more willing to start a conversation with a local than when you're with a friend.

How to do it: As a start, don't pay attention to those who consider the idea of traveling alone shocking. They're simply expressing their own fears and discomfort. Choose a route and activities that you really enjoy (maybe those you have no one to share with, anyway). A couple of ideas: a weekend at a village guest house, a yoga retreat, four to five days abroad, hiking through the mountains from one hut to the next, biking along small village roads + a tent, spa hotel for absolute relaxation, a bungalow on the shore of a lake.

For seasoned travelers: Spend time alone in a place you wouldn't normally go to, and do something you haven't done before. This will certainly stir up your peaceful life.

125.
Travel with a stranger

If you're not very communicative, this is a really serious challenge.

How to do it: If you're active on social media, join hiking groups or other theme groups dedicated to traveling. When they organize something, let them know you want to join. People in these groups are open to new encounters and, most probably, you will make a bunch of new friends before you know it. The other option is to ask friends and acquaintances if they can introduce you to people they know (for you, they will be strangers), or sign up to a tourist club.

Why do it: The stranger gives you a fresh perspective to a place, besides you're free to be yourself and show the best of you.

126.

Travel with someone you hardly know

Have you noticed how much traveling brings people together? Spend two days on the road with someone you don't know that well (a colleague; a distant acquaintance, somebody you've met once or twice) - usually this happens when you really want to go somewhere, but none of your closest companions are available. Then you find out that someone you hardly know is on the same wavelength as you and you tell yourself: why not? The hours spent in the car/on the train or along mountain trails will make you discuss topics you haven't touched upon before - and find things you have in common.

127.
Hitchhike

Often the first time people hitchhike, they do it because they're forced to (they missed the last bus, for instance), or they have run out of money, or they are young and free-spirited. If you haven't hitchhiked before, here are some basic pieces of advice:

1. Wait at a straight stretch of road - before and after a turn drivers don't have time to react, stop and pick you up.

2. Smile - no one wants Grumpy Cat in their car.

3. The best number of people to hitchhike is two. If you're alone - you arouse suspicion. If there's three of you - it's a crowd, split up.

4. To talk to the driver or keep silent? It depends on the person - you will sense it soon enough.

128.
Pick up a hitchhiker

Why do it: We will simply tell you a true story: "As I am wondering if I'm on the right way to the Treshtenik mountain hut, at a street just outside the town limits of Yakoruda in Bulgaria, I see two elderly ladies waving at me. So I wave back and take the opportunity to ask them if this is the right way. It turns out that they are not saying hello - they are hitchhiking. I pick up the two ladies - one of them with her grandson, the other with her man. They make themselves comfortable among the pile of maps and atlases, which slowly but surely takes over every inch of my car.

It takes two minutes to learn all that is important about the hut owner - his wife is a dentist, he has a small tractor... and also that the hut next to it belongs to Antoan, "a good man, though he comes too rarely." The two ladies are on their way to take care of the hay, high in the mountains. They hitchhike every day. And people say hitchhiking is dangerous?! - boy, did those ladies reach an old age!

As they get off, one of the elderly ladies throws a banknote on the seat and rushes out of the car (because she knows I won't take the money). The other one gives me final directions to the hut and wishes me a handsome man".

129.

Live abroad for a while - get more creative, richer and smarter

It seems that temporarily changing your residence not only recharges your batteries, but also makes you smarter, more creative and more attractive to employers. Not that people live abroad for these reasons, but the side effects prove more than favorable. Study abroad, participate in exchange programs or simply see what life is like in a favorite foreign country.

Why do it: Students who have lived abroad perform 18% better in solving problems, which require creativity (a study of a British university). People who have lived in a multicultural environment receive more job offers compared to those who have never lived abroad (a study of a big business school). Learning a foreign language develops the part of the brain which is responsible for memory (a Swedish study).

Get inspired... The Shuswap Native Americans lived a settled way of life. They could find everything they needed to survive near the village. However, with time, life became mundane, there were no challenges, everything was familiar and predictable, and so, once every 25-30 years the elders would take the decision for the whole village to move. That's how Native Americans found new rivers and new forests to explore. They found new challenges.

130.

Leave with an empty suitcase, come back with a full one

This is hardly the first time you've heard that phrase, but if you go on a holiday abroad with one empty suitcase, you will have enough space to put the presents for your close friends and family (and for yourself!).

131.

Bring back a pebble, some sand or another non-souvenir to remember the place by

As years go by, you will have a collection of pebbles, soil or pine-cones from hundreds of places around the world. Put a label next to each item in your collection.

Another idea is to collect in a jar sand or soil from the places you visit, pouring each on top of the previous and labelling the jar on the outside with the respective destination of origin.

132.

Find a solution to a problem... while you travel

You come back from a trip and a genius idea hits you! Sounds familiar? Well, it's not only you and it happens quite often - when you're in "traveling mode", your creativity usually heightens.

Why do it: When you have a problem to solve, traveling

is a great tool for two reasons. First, dopamine - a hormone, famous for its function to create a feeling of satisfaction in the brain. All activities that make us feel good and at the same time relaxed (like traveling, driving, even taking a shower), stimulate the brain's creativity. Traveling has another positive effect - distraction, a useful distraction. If you're stuck and feel unable to find a solution, taking a break may give you the necessary distance, at which your brain will be free from fixating on ineffective solutions.

133.

Create your own challenge - the crazier, the better

The world is full of crazy people who fulfil their own crazy challenges. Many of them are just looking for a reason not to stop in one place. Create your own freaky idea and set to accomplishing it.

Get inspired...

Matt Green - He sets himself the goal of walking every street in New York. He also keeps a blog to write about the little surprises and interesting people he encounters as he walks. It all began in 2011 and the challenge has continued for several years. More on imjustwalkin.com.

Graham Hughes - Graham managed to visit 201 countries and territories in the world, without even once taking a plane. His adventure has gone on for almost three years and included a short stay in a Congolese prison, an arrest in Russia and running in Iraq with a gun in his hand. Graham was given a Guinness World Record certificate as a record holder for visiting the most countries in a year without flying (130). More on theodysseyexpedition.com.

Dixe Wills set himself the goal of visiting every place in Great Britain whose name begins with the letter "Z".

The total number is 41. He managed to do it within a year. Then he wrote a book, entitled "The Z-Z of Great Britain". After he completed this challenge, Dixe traveled Great Britain's entire sea coast by catching local buses only - 196 buses in six and a half weeks. More on dixewills.com.

Other ideas: Climb every peak on the nearest mountain. Visit all villages that begin with the letter of your first name and take a picture with the village sign. Eat fresh pasta in every town in Italy.

Your personal crazy challenge:

. . . .

134.

The 12-month challenge

We challenge you to take up a challenge every month of the year.

January - Try a new meal for the first time.

February - Accept an offer you would normally turn down.

March - Learn something new while you travel (to take photos, taste wine, new stories, new recipes).

April - Take a nap under a tree in blossom.

May - Share an adventure with a friend.

June - Do something you haven't done before.

July - Do something extreme.

August - Try absolute relaxation - go offline.

September - Plan a big trip.

October - Visit a destination you've been dreaming about for a long time.

November - Go in an unknown direction, leave things to chance.

December - Send someone on a trip to give them the gift of traveling.

135.

Give a second chance to a destination you didn't like the first time

Just because the first time you were in Paris, it was raining cats and dogs and you got a flat tyre right in the middle of the intersection during rush hour, it doesn't mean that Paris is a soaking-wet disaster for tourists. In fact, it means that you got a flat tyre in the rain and nothing more. It also means that it's worth going back with an umbrella and a spare tyre to find the beauty in the city.

Smart travelers don't make general assumptions based on one experience and are always open to second and third chances.

Which is the destination you didn't like at first:

. . . .

When did you give it a second chance?

. . . .

136.
The most difficult challenge for active people

If you're one of those people who is always on the move, busy doing something, talking to someone, planning something... here's your biggest challenge. Spend a whole day doing nothing. Rest, observe the world around you, take a nap in the afternoon, have a cup of tea... Genuinely try to enjoy doing nothing.

The day you spent doing absolutely nothing (date, where were you and how did it make you feel):

. . . .

137.
Go on a journey back to your roots

"A child on a farm sees a plane fly overhead and dreams of a faraway place. A traveler on the plane sees the farmhouse... and thinks of home."

—Carl Burns

Travel miles looking for the places, where your ancestors lived to learn more about yourself.

A couple of ideas:

1. Ask your grandparents to tell you about their childhood.

2. Record the story so that you can see and hear them even when they depart this life.

3. Go to the places where they grew up and do some of the things they used to do.

4. Do some research and complete the family tree.

5. Look for relatives you've never met. Introduce yourself and get to know them.

HOME-TOWN CHALLENGES

Use this chapter:

1. *When you feel bored in your own town.*

2. *When you can't travel far.*

3. *When you think you know everything about your town.*

138.
Go where you've been numerous times before

...and don't leave until you find out at least five new things/stories/people.

It's very possible this challenge will be among the last ones in the book you complete. Probably because we suggest you go where you think you know everything. The idea of the challenge is to show you that you might miss a lot by thinking you know everything.

How to do it: The easiest way is to imagine that you're going there for the first time. Look for the details, talk to people, ask questions you know the answers to (often, the answers you get are unexpected).

The place you visited:

. . . .

Findings:

. . . .

139.

Go to the rooftop of a building and see the city from above

When in a foreign place, tourists are ready to pay significant amounts of money to go up the Empire State Building or other observation decks upon skyscrapers. They don't do it in their own town, though, where the pleasure is most probably free. Even if there are no skyscrapers around, find a tall building where a friend of yours works or lives, go to its rooftop and have a lemonade while enjoying the view.

140.

Put a message in a bottle

This rather romantic gesture isn't very eco-friendly, not to mention that too many rivers unfortunately carry so many bottles that it's unlikely anyone will open yours and read the message inside. That's why, instead of throwing one more bottle in a river or sea, leave the message at a more strategic place - in the park, in the foyer of a public building, etc. Tell your story or pay forward the most positive lesson life has taught you. It's surprising how therapeutic this can be both for you and the person who will read your message.

Get inspired... by a true story. In 1956 a Swedish sailor named Ake Viking, suffering from a lack of love in his life, started looking for a companion with the help of salty waters. He wrote a message to "someone beautiful and far away", tucked it into a bottle and tossed it in the sea. Two years later he received an answer from a Sicilian named Paolina: "I am not beautiful, but it seems so miraculous that this little bottle should have traveled so far and long to reach me that I must send you an answer". The two started exchanging letters and eventually Viking moved to Sicily to marry the woman that the sea had chosen for him.

141.
Go far away from the city at night to gaze at the stars

City lights prevent you from seeing the sky in all its splendour. Go a few miles out of town and you will see so many more constellations. Take a blanket to lie on the ground comfortably.

How to make it more interesting: Download a constellation identifying app (like Sky Map, for example). Find Mars, Venus, Saturn, the Zodiac constellations.

142.

Have dinner in an exotic restaurant (*Indian, Thai, Armenian, etc.*)

It's a culinary trip in itself, with no passport needed.

143.

Get up really early and practice your favorite sport outside before work

Too few people will be thrilled when they read a challenge starting with "get up really early". The truth is, exactly this kind of early rising will make you feel so refreshed that you will certainly want to do it again some time.
If you think that coffee is refreshing, try at least once mountain biking early in the morning on a weekday, only to see how fresh and full of energy you can feel at work, even if you got up at 5:30 am.

A couple of ideas (tested): In winter, when the fresh snow falls during the night, take the skis or snowboard and go up the nearest slope to enjoy the snow powder with a slide down. Tell your boss that, due to personal reasons, you will be late to work by an hour or two. In summer, cycle in the mountains. If you prefer more relaxed activities, go to a beautiful place outside town and do yoga or try gokotta (*See Challenge 39*).

144.
Walk to work

If you usually go to work by crowded public transport or by car, choose a nice sunny day and go to work on foot.

How to do it: Look on an online map what the distance to your office is. When not in a hurry, people usually walk at a speed of 5 kph (3 mph). If you live 6 km (3 mi) from your workplace - it will take you about 70 minutes. Get up earlier than usual. Plan time for a coffee or a breakfast break on the way (you can prepare breakfast at home and eat it in a nice park). Choose your route so that you pass through as many parks and quiet streets as possible - thus walking to work will be a genuinely refreshing and recharging experience.

A couple more ideas: If you walk to work anyway, change your usual route. Take different streets every day for several consecutive days, even if it means walking a bit further, or get up earlier than usual and do some sport before work (*See Challenge 143*)

145.
Go to a massage

Many people indulge in a massage when on holiday (on the beach, under the palm trees or in a spa hotel). It has so many benefits for the body and soul that it's worth booking a massage appointment right away, without waiting for the next vacation. We will mention just a few of its benefits - it decreases levels of depression and anxiety, strengthens the immune system, improves sleep and sharpens focus.

146.

Get on the public transport and get off at the last stop

Pick a bus/tram/subway line whose route you don't know well. Discover new neighborhoods, interesting places or people. Take at least half an hour to explore before you leave.

147.

A challenge on a gloomy, rainy or cold weekend

Rainy weather is actually not bad weather. Apart from giving you the chance to stop for a while, it might also be very good... not to stop. If you feel restless, but the weather is not exactly what you'd call "nice", here's what you can do:

A couple of ideas:

Go to a museum (have you visited them all?) or a gallery - it's not raining there.

Visit a cave - it's not raining there, either.

Make a video with the photos from your favorite trips.

Add your favorite music.

Eat in a restaurant serving foreign cuisine.

Invite friends over and cook a theme dinner (Greek, Italian, Indian).

Watch travel movies.

Read a book about faraway places.

Arrange the photos from previous trips.

Do some research and plan the next trip.

Go to a massage parlor/spa center or try another relaxing activity.

Travel by train.

Catch up on sleep.

Make love.

Try indoor climbing, dancing or yoga.

Go outside and jump into puddles.

148.
Notice the pine cone

"He to whom the emotion is a stranger, who can no longer pause to wonder and stand wrapped in awe, is as good as dead - his eyes are closed"

—Albert Einstein

Or how to really be present, wherever you are - be there not only physically but mentally and with all your heart. If you're just opening on this page and you're wondering what to do, here's something that is as simple as it is hard to do - stop, look around and find something beautiful around you. It could be an ordinary pine cone. As Buddhists say: "Do not dwell in the past, do not dream of the future, concentrate the mind on the present moment."

Why do it: According to a study conducted in 2003 (Isaacowitz, Vaillant, and Seligman), people who regularly make time to notice the beauty around them turn out to be 12% more satisfied with life in general. People very quickly get used to the beautiful things that surround them (the scientific term is hedonic adaptation) and they need to make a deliberate effort to notice and appreciate them all over again, instead of taking them for granted. For example, you take your health for granted until you get sick, etc.

How to do it: Stop and look up (regardless of whether you're in the forest or in the city) - we tend to forget to look beyond our own self. Notice the rays of sunlight shining through the leaves. Feel the wind touching your skin. See the nuances of the buildings changing with the setting sun. Stop and sense the fragrances right at that moment. Notice the shapes of the clouds and what they remind you of.

149.

Visit a temple of a religion, other than yours (*if you're an atheist — pick one of the many*)

When you're on a holiday abroad, you visit mosques, Buddhist temples, synagogues…, but you don't do it in your own country. Have you ever thought of that? Pick a temple of a religion different from your own and learn something about its history. It could be a church, mosque, synagogue, a temple of an ancient civilization…

150.

Go wine tasting

Wineries, wine bars and specialized wine shops often organize themed wine tastings, combined with nibbles and interesting stories related to wine.

151.

Go to a live performance of a new/unfamiliar band

Because you might like them, even though you haven't heard of them before. Because it will liven up your evening. Because it is something different.

152.

Check into a hotel in your own town

Check into a boutique hotel, a cute guest house, a winery or spa hotel in your own town. Pick a special weekend when you will recharge your batteries not by traveling long distances, but by choosing to leave all worries aside - from what you will have for dinner to wondering whether to change the sheets or not...

153.
Pretend to be a tourist in your own town

Stop people on the street and ask them for directions to the city attractions (for seasoned travelers: in a foreign language because you're Hungarian/Dutch/Ethiopian). Ask about the most interesting places in town where they'd recommend eating. Who knows, you might learn something new! You can thank them in the end and, if you want, tell them about the challenge.

Why do it: There are things you take for granted and the town you live in is one of them. This challenge will give you a fresh perspective and will surely introduce you to some interesting people.

FRIENDSHIP AND LOVE CHALLENGES

Challenges to complete with your friends. Many are suitable for your loved ones, your parents, team building with colleagues, and other forms of human relationships. But before that...

The importance of traveling with your friends

A 75-year-long Harvard study on what makes people happier and healthier traces hundreds of individual lives year after year from the 1930s up to this day. It concludes that the most important factor for good health, long life and happiness is the relationships we have with other people - family, friends and even acquaintances and neighbors. Those who have someone to rely on in a difficult moment, who foster their relationships with close ones, are healthier, have fewer memory problems, live longer and are more satisfied with life. The fourth study director, Robert Waldinger, shares in an interview several ideas on how we can work towards strengthening our relationships with others: "Replace screen time with people time. Reach out to someone you haven't spoken to in years. Liven up a stale relationship by doing something new together - long walks or date nights, for example..."

154.

Send a paper postcard by post

Do you enjoy receiving postcards? One of those old-time cardboard postcards you need a stamp for, not an internet connection. The next time you travel to another city or abroad, send a real paper postcard from a real post office.

How to do it: Write down your friends' and relatives' addresses in advance. Sign the postcards and send them by post. Even if they arrive after you've already come back, the gesture will be appreciated.
If you're reading this challenge and you don't know a single address, you can send a postcard to yourself. Write a special message and expect mail when you get back home.

Get inspired... Did you know you can receive a postcard from a stranger on the other side of the world? There's a website - postcrossing.com, that brings together postcard lovers from 203 countries. After you register, the site randomly provides the address of another user to send a postcard to. You can fill in some brief information about yourself and what postcards you prefer (landscape or city postcards, with people or flowers, signed or not, in an envelope, with a poem, signed in the local language...). Thus the postcard may include a very personal message, like: "Greetings to you and your three children. Hoping it's not too cold in Siberia".

155.

Sunrise and a morning picnic

Get in your car and drive at night. Go to the beach or another beautiful place to watch the sunrise. Watch the sun coming up with friends or your loved one. Have a picnic in the morning and then take a short nap on the blanket.

156.

Trust a friend to organize your trip

Set a budget and leave the organizational side to a close friend. It could be a surprise - in the end, you simply receive an envelope with reservations, GPS coordinates and a list of the necessary luggage. You in turn organize the next trip for a friend.

157.

Spend a day at a theme park

Try everything, no exceptions - from cotton candy to a merry-go-round and shooting games.

158.

Create a short movie from your trip

Make videos of yourself, of landscapes or of interesting people you've met. Then compile all the videos in one short movie. If you're very much into it, add the songs you listened to on the road. There are plenty of free and easy to use programs to help you compile movies.

159.

Sign your trip photos with funny remarks

Choose the funniest photos from the trip and get creative.

How to do it: If you want to label simply the pictures or add arrows, Christmas trees and other basic changes, you can try an easy-to-use intuitive program (PhotoScape is free and easy, Pixlr is similar to Photoshop and can be used for free online). If you have no problem working with Photoshop, you can even send your friends to Hawaii or into space.

160.

Print a photo of the person who can't join you on the trip

If someone in the group can't come on the long-planned Oktoberfest trip... well, you've got nothing else to do but print their head on a piece of cardboard (real life-size would be best) and glue it to a stick. Then take a picture of the friend who stayed behind (of their hapless printed head, that is) in front of every attraction, beer and Bavarian girl, and send them the pictures in real time.

161.

Travel by unusual means of transport

Choose a means of transport you haven't traveled with before and see the world differently. You don't have to buy anything, just hire it for a day. Travel in a group.

A couple of ideas: A bike, electric bike, scooter, motorcycle, convertible, carriage, boat.

162.

Have a barbecue

The good thing about barbecues is that there's something for everyone - some like to prepare a super, special marinade for the meat, others to start the barbecue fire, grill sausages or cook the perfect potatoes and ember-roasted corn. There's always this guy who never does much, but whose never-ending jokes crack everyone up.

163.

Do a good deed

The world is full of people and animals who need help, and the Internet is full of information about them. Choose a cause that is important to you, get organized and visit a place where you can do a good deed. You will see a new place, meet new people and feel satisfied all at once. The people you're helping will feel refreshed and optimistic to see not one but a whole group of people willing to help out.

164.

Finally get round to visiting that friend who lives in another town or country

You certainly have at least one friend or relative living abroad, who's been asking you to go and visit for years. It's one thing to receive an invitation, to take it up is another. Proceed to the second part - you will make a close friend happy, who is perhaps lonely, plus you will see a new place.

Who should I finally visit:

. . . .

165.
Game of opposites

Make the most of the time spent in the car/on the train, playing this simple game which often leads to unexpected turn of events. Someone says a sentence and another has to contradict them. For instance: James: "Luckily, we have plenty of food in the car". John: "Unfortunately, all of it has gone bad", etc.

166.

Before going on a trip together, compile a themed playlist

It's a proven fact that music tends to remind us of the places we heard it for the first time.

How to do it: If you're going abroad, find the Top 40 most popular current songs as well as some evergreen classics. When you arrive, listen to a local radio station in the car or on your smartphone. Use song recognizing apps (like Shazam) to see the artist and the name of the songs you like on the local radio. Later they will bring you back to your trip.

167.

Take home a recipe instead of a souvenir

You can't always bring back fridge magnets. Your friends' refrigerator doors will fall off soon! So instead of keychains, postcards and different gadgets, next time, bring your friends a foreign recipe. If someone's been to Zanzibar recently, invite the others over for dinner, cook local meals, show pictures and tell stories.

How to do it:

1. Find a local. Who'll teach you to prepare a better tiramisu than a 55-year-old Italian lady who's been serving it her whole life as dessert for Sunday lunch? If you know someone or know someone who knows someone abroad, make sure you get a dinner invitation, or better yet ask to go over earlier with a bottle of wine and help with the cooking.

2. Find a local snack bar. If step one is not applicable, look for a local snack bar. Not a restaurant. These unpretentious food bars are a source of the most authentic cuisine following recipes that locals have known since they were little. If you can't guess what's in your dish, express your admiration to the cook and ask to have the ingredients of the meal written down. You can translate them later.

3. Shop away. If any of the ingredients are difficult to find in your country, don't forget to buy them before you go back.

4. Cook. Here comes the sweetest part: when you get back, invite your friends over for dinner and cook the recipes you brought. It's a perfect occasion to see one another, have something to eat, share some interesting stories about hunting foreign delicacies. If dinner doesn't work out the first time, fear not - it's still another story to tell!

A couple of ideas: If you and your friends have traveled significant distances together, why not gather from time to time at dinner to enjoy the funny pictures from mutual trips - the time spent going through old photos as well as reminiscing about the events will be refreshing. You can also have a themed dinner devoted to a destination you haven't been to but you'd very much like to visit (Polynesia, anyone?).

168.

Come up with new names to use while you're abroad

Stephanie and John in the Netherlands are Stefana and Johann, in Romania - Stefania and Ion, in Italy - Stefania and Giovanni. The names could be completely different from your own. For example, after passing the border, Peter automatically becomes Stewart, Ana is now Martha - only the customs officers checking your passports will know the truth.

If you're camping or in the mountains, come up with funny scout names according to your personality - The Big Berry, The Quick Hatchet, The Eagle Eye, etc.

169.

Go to the concert of a favorite band abroad

For concert tourists it's a double win - they listen to their favorite artists live and visit new places. Check regularly the websites of your favorite bands for concert dates in countries you'd like to go to anyway.

170.

Send someone else on a trip

The best present for a close friend is a trip.

Why do it: It's a proven fact that buying experiences brings much more satisfaction than buying material things. One recent study (*Kumar, Killingsworth, Gilovich, Psychol Sci., 2014*) shows that experiential purchases make people happy for longer periods. The motto "live for the moment" is quite popular today, but living in anticipation of this moment turns out to be even better. It's the anticipation before and the memories after the experience itself that create the longer positive effect. That's why traveling, concerts, movies, theater performances are better gifts than material things.

At first glance, this is what seems logical: if you give a vacation as a present, the person will go, then come back and it will be over; but if you give them a material thing, it will remain. In reality, however, people tend to very quickly get used to new items and stop appreciating their belongings if they see and use them all the time. It's not like that with experiences - they are either too short to get used to, or time "cleans up" any negative details from our memories and they become more and more pleasant in our minds.

171.

Enthuse a friend with your hobbies

If you're into rock climbing, take a friend to a beginner's class. If you like skiing, invite a friend to the slopes for a weekend to show them the first moves. If you enjoy traveling alone, get on the train with a friend and sit in different compartments. When you arrive, each of you sees the city on their own for an hour (or two, or three). After that you meet and discuss your separate experiences.

172.

Smile for a picture on the road and send it to a friend you haven't traveled with for a long time

Add something like "I thought of you. We should go again some time, just like when…"

Why do it: Studies show that when you take a picture of yourself to send to someone else, both the recipient and the sender feel positive emotions. Long live the selfie!

173.

Visit a friend without being invited

Bring something to drink and the ingredients for a recipe to cook together. It's enough to call and check if your friend is home and if they have a couple of free hours. The rest is a surprise.

(Caution! After this challenge was written and shared with some of this book's team members, the first reaction of some

of them was: "Oh, that's terrible!" We're not saying you shouldn't do it, but choose carefully who you can apply it to!).

174.
Take a friend on a surprise trip

Saturday is coming. You're thinking where to go... and you think and you think... but you're not getting anywhere... Sound familiar? If yes, now is the time to organize an unforgettable trip for a friend.

How to do it: You know that the person in question is in a "new places" mode. Now you only have to choose the place and provide basic information: where and what time you meet, what your friend needs to bring (depending on the plan - comfortable shoes, sandwiches, binoculars, hammock, pink scarf). Show up at the appointed time and in solemn silence take your friend to your transport. For a stronger effect, prepare a special experience at the place (horseback riding, meeting with an interesting person, etc.). Sounds like a birthday surprise? It doesn't have to be their birthday to make them feel special!

175.

Hitchhike to see who will arrive first

Choose a final destination and split up to hitchhike alone or in teams. The first to arrive wins, the rest - well, their treat.

176.

Plan a secret trip

Don't tell anyone where you're going and what you're going to do. Keep everything as a great secret. When someone asks, just exchange knowing looks. Tell your friends only after you come back. (Many people are forced to apply this technique when they have to tell their mothers they're going on a trip to Kosovo, Afghanistan or a similarly less celebrated destination).

177.

Find the most delicious pizza (*steak, burger*)

Include an important mission in your trip - to find the most delicious pizza, steak, burger, etc.

How to do it:
You can create a strict evaluation system including different criteria (taste, aroma, service) and everyone gives a score from 1 to 10. You can divide Rome into neighborhoods and split up to look for the best gelato (ice-cream) until you find it or catch a cold.

178.
Make a list of the destinations for the year

It doesn't have to be around New Year - no matter when you're reading this challenge, ask your friends to write down several destinations they'd like to visit by the end of the year. Combine them all in one list and start checking them off together.

179.
Take a picture at the same place every year

It's a wonderful tradition which maintains friendships, reminds you to travel and gives you a reason to see your friends more regularly (even when different things in your life separate you for longer periods). You can pick a day that is important to everyone - somebody's birthday, New Year's Eve, etc.

180.

Go to a carnival

Having fun at a carnival is the best way to unleash your party spirit. Carnivals appeared hundreds of years ago as a way of shedding inhibitions, and today they do exactly this. You will see your friends in a different light; unstoppable and free.

181.

Create a special tradition on the road

Traditions are the best thing about friendships (besides the fact you can call someone at 3 am without even thinking!). Create a special tradition on the road.

A couple of ideas: Some traveling companions have a mascot (a toy), others have the tradition of bringing waffles from faraway lands instead of magnets, others start every trip with the same song.

182.

Use your friends to help you step outside of your comfort zone

"Wanna taste grasshoppers on a stick?", "Shall we jump into the sea off those cliffs over there?". When you hesitate whether to do something you wouldn't normally do, it's always great to have someone beside you who will shrug their shoulders and say "Why not?". Friends who travel together derive energy and inspiration from one another. So it's always a good idea to take the craziest of your friends with you, if you want to be the bravest you can be.

183.

Organize a free trip

Now that you know the world is full of free things (see Challenge 94), use this knowledge to organize a trip at a time you're all short on cash. Your budget doesn't have to be 0, but you can set the goal of realizing the cheapest trip possible in your life. Plus the efforts to get the lowest price will surely create a number of funny situations.

How to do it: Choose the cheapest transport (hitchhiking, bike, train, public transport). Bring homemade food. Take advantage of the free museum admissions on the respective days.

184.
Go to a place, where there's absolutely nothing interesting

We know that you can go off the map to a place where there's only wind rocking straws and prickles, and still have a great day just because you're with friend(s). Take your most adventurous friend with you (or maybe that's you in your group?) and ask them to complete this challenge - to have a great time where there's absolutely nothing.

How to do it: Take funny photos in the wilderness. Find interesting plants and animals. The fact that there's nothing to distract you means that you will have plenty of time to talk about anything and everything.

185.
Ask a friend to challenge you to do something at the place you're going to

Make your trip even more interesting by asking your friends to come up with a challenge. In Brazil - play football with the locals on the beach, take a picture with a toucan, drink coconut water with a straw right from the coconut; in Cuba - have a cigar at the sea boulevard Malecon... If someone finds it difficult, they can always open this book on a random page for inspiration.

Take the list of challenges with you and don't come back until you've completed them all. Trying to fulfil them will introduce you to interesting people and will put you in unexpected situations (tested on a number of occasions by the authors of this book).

CRAZY CHALLENGES

"If at some point you don't ask yourself, 'What have I gotten myself into?' then you're not doing it right."

—Roland Gau

"Twenty years from now you will be more disappointed by the things that you didn't do than by the ones you did do. So throw off the bowlines. Sail away from the safe harbor. Catch the trade winds in your sails. Explore. Dream. Discover."

—Mark Twain

186.

Have breakfast at home. Have lunch 300 km (200 mi) away. Have dinner abroad.

And then share the experience in three photos.

Why share: Because it's proven that positive posts on Facebook are "contagious" - every share of positive news/facts/photos leads to another two positive posts among your friends.

187.

Go to the airport and buy a ticket for the cheapest destination of the day

Go to the airport with your luggage packed. You can go together with your friends. The destination is not important. Spend the weekend there.

188.

Swim in a pool of beer
(*or wine, or green tea*)

A beer pool? A wine bath? It's not only in your dreams.

A couple of ideas:

The Austrian brewery Starkenberger is the first in the world to fill a huge empty space with beer and invite its visitors to feel like gods. There is a total of seven pools, each filled with 12 000 liters (3170 gal) of water mixed

with 300 liters (79 gal) of yeast sediment. For maximum comfort the pools are heated and the environment resembles that of a Turkish bath. The two-hour swim isn't dry at all - it includes beer (not from the pool, of course) and some bites to accompany the drink. You need to book the beer swim in advance. The brewery is near the town of Tarrenz, about 60 km (38 mi) from Innsbruck.

Yunessun Spa Resort in Japan, famous for its mineral springs, boasts not only warm mineral pools but also pools of red wine, green tea and sake.

Fun fact: Bathing in beer has been considered healing and relaxing ever since Cleopatra did it in the absence of Marc Antony (although they say Cleopatra bathed in almost anything, so we'll let this one slide and will accept it as pure truth).

189.
Spend a weekend in the wilderness without bringing food or a tent

Mountain tourism is incredibly popular today, partly because there is equipment, tents and waterproof clothes available for even the most casual mountaineer. If you're in adventure mode, however, spend two days close to nature without all that. Forage for food and water in nature, build a shelter, start a fire without matches or a lighter (*see how - Challenge 29*). Be a true survivor.

190.

Go to a big bookstore and leave notes in your favorite travel books for future readers.

191.

Take a camera and a pair of rubber boots

Make a photo story about a day in the life of an invisible man.

192.

Make a raft and sail along a river

There are plenty of tutorials on the Internet to show you how to build a raft. Now you only have to put it together and sail it down a river.

193.

Join the ice-cold New Year's Dive in the Netherlands (*and other icy ideas*)

1st January in the Netherlands is no time for lying around and sobering up in front of the TV, but for the traditional New Year's plunge into the icy waters of the sea, lakes and rivers. More than 25,000 Dutch people take part in this refreshing procedure every year. The largest dive is held at the beach of Scheveningen - a seaside region in the Hague, where about 10,000 people plunge into the sea each year.

A couple more ideas: A traditional icy dive is held on Christmas day in Serpentine Lake (Hyde Park, London). In North America there are 'polar bear' clubs that organize charity ice dives. In Russia and other Orthodox countries, on the day of the revelation of God (Epiphany, 6th or 19th January) an iron cross is cast into the icy waters of a river. Young men race to retrieve it. It is believed that the first who reaches the cross will be healthy and happy all year long.

194.
Find the world's largest... whatever

Everything that exists has its LARGEST version somewhere around the world. Whether you're looking for the largest pumpkin, the largest aquapark, the highest observation deck, this will be a challenge full of dangers and adventures. Do you accept the challenge?
You can also look for the tiniest, most visited, ugliest, most ancient... whatever.

195.
Lost and found couples challenge

Go on a vacation with your loved one in a faraway city. Once you arrive, split up and try to find each other. The biggest question is how you will play the game: whether you will do what you usually do so that your partner can find you; or you will look for activities you think your partner will be doing? Romantic cities with compact city centers (like Vienna, Bratislava and Amsterdam) are a good option.

196.

Invite strangers over for dinner

Go to a stranger's house for dinner or sit at a table with other strangers who haven't met one another before.

"Secret Supper" (or "Supper Club") is a culinary trend that's getting more and more popular in Europe and North America. This is a great way to meet new people, travel, explore new worlds and tastes.

The rules are simple - you put your name on a waiting list and, on particular days, complete strangers sit at the hosts' table. The hosts do the cooking, guests bring wine and split the money for the groceries. The place where the dinner will take place remains a secret until you receive the invitation for the respective date. Google "hidden supper" or "secret supper" + the name of a town. Or start organizing secret suppers yourself.

197.
Ski or snowboard only in your underwear.

Or even without.

198.

Go to a town you don't know. Ring a random doorbell and give the person who answers your favorite book as a present

Explain that this is a challenge from a book and that if they want, they can do the same thing.

199.

Get in the car — turn right then left. Repeat. Again... and again...

Don't stop until you find something interesting. Take pictures along the way.

200.

Join one of the craziest festivals in the world

If you feel like doing something really crazy, there are hundreds of festivals around the world created just for people like you.

A couple of ideas:

La Tomatina (Spain) - This is the biggest tomato fight. Every year, thousands of tomato fans arrive in the village of Buñol, close to Valencia, to take part in the epic tomato fight - La Tomatina. More than 30,000 people wait impatiently for the flare signalling the start the fight, and several trucks haul the tomatoes used in the fight. It takes place on the last Wednesday in August.

Burning Man (USA) - This festival is a must for every free spirit. It's hard to put into words, so you have to be there to understand what exactly this event is all about. For two weeks each year, tens of thousands of people gather in the desert near the city of Reno, USA, to create a temporary metropolis dedicated to exchanging knowledge, skills, creativity and art. Nothing is sold, there are only acts of gift giving. The culmination of the event is the symbolic ritual burning of a large wooden effigy - "the Man", from whence comes the name of the festival.

Holi - festival of colors (India) - Every year during this joyful festival, the streets of Indian towns fill with people who throw colored powder and colored water at each other. No one gets out dry and uncolored! The holiday is dedicated to fertility. The date varies, it's usually in March.

Songkran - Wet New Year (Thailand) - The Thai New Year, celebrated on 13th April, has turned into great fun for locals and visitors. The Thai people pay reverence to Buddha, clean their houses and pour water over elders as a way to show respect. Over the past years, though, the tradition has become a bit wilder - whether you're an elder or not, expect water gun shoot-outs in the streets, whole buckets of water to be amicably poured over you or water balloons to be thrown at you.

Up Helly Aa (Scotland) - This is the name of the biggest fire-Viking creation of Scotland. A festival where every year a whole galley (Viking long ship) is burnt down. In the Scottish town of Lerwick there is a procession of burning torches and the term "Viking drinking spree" acquires whole new dimensions. It's always held on the last Tuesday of January.

Menton Lemon Festival (France) - In February the French Riviera will surprize you with a refreshing dose of vitamin C - a three-week, open-air festival, where scantily-clad dancers move to the rhythm of Brazilian music among huge sculptures of oranges and lemons. Each statue takes weeks to make, and the theme is different every year - from an round-the-world trip to Disneyland to antique heroes.

201.
Make a photomontage from a trip that never actually happened

Watch the reactions when you show the photos. Decide whether and when to reveal the truth.

202.
The most important challenge: Give up something

Challenges are everywhere around you - especially within you. You want to see the Northern Lights, learn how to surf, walk in the jungle with the gorillas, speak Swahili and Mandarin, swim with sharks and climb the Great Wall of China... but you're terrified that one life won't be enough to do all that. Sounds familiar?

In fact, you're right. One life won't be enough. Take this as the biggest challenge of all. Challenge others and accept their challenges, but you need to understand that if you don't succeed in something - it's not the end of the world. Maybe you set too many goals. Maybe you started too many things and left them unfinished. And maybe you are investing all your energy into thousands of ideas instead of focusing on several important ones.

And do you know the secret to completing more goals from your list of dream destinations (and the list of life goals for that matter)? To give up a few of them. This way you won't live under the constant pressure of failed attempts, and you will have enough energy to concentrate on realizing several of the things. When you're done with them, you can continue with the rest.

10 incredibly simple ways to be happy on the road

1. Stop comparing yourself with others and where they go.

2. Do only what you love. You usually have too little time at a certain place to explore somebody else's destinations.

3. If something goes wrong - don't be quick to get angry. Maybe something better came into its place.

4. Big expectations are the greatest obstacle to appreciating what you have.

5. Be here and now. Don't think about yesterday and tomorrow.

6. Instead of souvenirs, collect experiences, friends and beautiful memories.

7. Accept that not everything was made for you to be comfortable. In fact, it's made for the locals to be comfortable.

8. What you think is wrong, might be normal here. Everything "normal" has its geographical borders.

9. Don't stick strictly to the plan - allow some detours.

10. Accept acts of hospitality. Someone in the street invites you to have a coffee? Accept. That's how the greatest stories (and friendships) are created.

203.
GAME: Discover a new city

Take a dice, coin or whatever tiny thing you have at hand and roll it over the game section "Discover a new city". Complete the challenge on which the dice fell.

Learn the origin of the city's name.

Find a place or person with an interesting story (street, famous city resident, urban legend). Search for additional information on the topic.

Share a bottle of local wine at sunset.

Get lost (on purpose).

Find a place with a magnificent view. Try to remember what you see, hear, smell and touch.

Find a place that overlooks the city.

Go to a busy market or flea market. Haggle over prices.

Take a random bus and get off at a random stop. Walk around for at least 30 minutes before you head back.

Go to a concert/opera/live performance in a bar or restaurant.

Have a picnic in the park.

Find a free event that takes place today and go there (ask at the local tourist center or the hotel).

Sit on a bench and watch the passersby. Come up with stories about some of them.

Try a local drink (tea, exotic fruit juice, beer).

Talk to the next stranger you see (What's the time? Do you live here? Recommend us a place with a beautiful view.). Try to keep up the conversation longer.

Eat something you haven't tried before.

ACKNOWLEDGEMENTS

For the ideas, inspiration and support for these challenges, we would like to thank: Ivalina Nenova, Alexander Nenov, Marina Garbeva, Albena Ivanova, Bozhidar Bonchev, Asen Nenov, Alexandra Dimitrova, Nikolina Ruskova, James Crouchman, Irina Peneva, Nevena Nikolova, Lachezar Sokolov, Georgi Kyuchukov, Lucy Mallows.